Student Athletes: Shattering the Myths and Sharing the Realities

Edited by

Wyatt D. Kirk, EdD
Sarah V. Kirk, PhD

Rock Valley College
Educational Resources
Center

AMERICAN
COUNSELING
ASSOCIATION

5999 Stevenson Avenue
Alexandria, VA 22304-3300

American Counseling Association
5999 Stevenson Avenue
Alexandria, VA 22304

Cover design by Sarah Jane Valdez

Library of Congress Cataloging-in-Publication Data

Student athletes : shattering the myths and sharing the realities /
  edited by Wyatt D. Kirk, Sarah V. Kirk.
      p.   cm.
  Includes bibliographical references and index.
  ISBN 1-55620-098-6
    1. School sports—Social aspects—United States.   2. College
  sports—Social aspects—United States.   3. College athletes—
  United States.   I. Kirk, Sarah V.   II. Kirk, Wyatt D.
  GV346.S78 1993   92-18721
  306.4′83′0973—dc20   CIP

Printed in the United States of America

*This book is dedicated to
my daughter Kimberly Kirk-Jennings and
my son the Reverend Stephen S. Kirk*

and

*to all the future athletes
who may benefit from
this treatise.*

— WDK

*To the memory of my parents
Dr. and Mrs. David C. Virgo (Velmon E.)
as well as my extended family
throughout the world.*

— SVK

CONTENTS

that show just how these systems can and have worked, and it highlights athletes who have benefited from them.

In the United States today more than 20 million children participate in youth sports programs. Many will need special attention and assistance to maximize their full potential—academically, athletically, and emotionally. Fortunately there are more people than ever dedicated to helping. *Student Athletes: Shattering the Myths and Sharing the Realities* provides immeasurable support in that effort. Congratulations are in order to the Kirks and all the contributors for this excellent publication.

— Richard E. Lapchick

PREFACE

Few issues in America have received as much public attention during the last 5 to 10 years as has the world of athletics. The evidence is becoming clear and overwhelming to the majority of our society that there is some type of serious problem in athletics today. We are also hearing from all sectors of the sports world itself, and from the media, that something is wrong in intercollegiate athletics. The United States Congress has decided it is time to investigate the seriousness of the problem and has authored at least six different legislative bills to correct abuses and/or reform intercollegiate athletics. A number of commissions and task forces from all levels of the sports community are also studying the situation. Most now concede that many of the difficulties have arisen because top leaders in the sports world have failed to recognize the magnitude of the challenges facing them. Many of the reforms deal only with the symptoms and not with the real causes.

This book is designed to bring together some of the information available on academics and athletics, and to discuss some of the areas of concern in professional sports as well. Each chapter will feature some of the myths and realities surrounding the topic developed by the author. The insightful overviews of major issues will assist in underscoring the challenges that human service workers must face as they strive to better understand and maximize the positives between academics and athletes. This understanding is necessary if our young men and women are to be helped. The book's projected audience includes counselors, psychologists, social workers, coaches, academic advisors, parents, and the athletes themselves. It will also be an appropriate resource for those involved in sports medicine, recreation, and other areas of sports life.

The book is divided into three major parts. Part I (chapters 1 through 6) describes the athletic environment and the athlete's participation in it. Part II (chapters 7 through 11) explores a number of special issues within the athletic environment. Part III (chapters 12 through 15) examines external issues that have an impact on athletics. Finally, case examples are presented to provide a better understanding and appreciation of the issues discussed in this book.

OVERVIEW OF CONTENTS

Part I: The Athletic Environment

Chapters 1 through 6 describe the environment's impact on the student athlete. Included in this section is information on the roles of parents, mentors, coaches, and counselors during the athlete's formative years. These persons can make the difference in the athlete's overall development and self-enhancement.

In chapter 1, "Developmental Benefits of Athletics," Mary Mitchell Harris addresses the impact of athletics, both positive and negative, on young people during the little league, high school, and college years. She sets a positive tone by debunking some of the myths surrounding student athletes and urging their acceptance as students—no better than and no less than their colleagues. She recommends the power learning model, based on her research, as a viable tool in working with them.

In chapter 2, "School Counseling and the Student Athlete," Beverly J. O'Bryant provides information from the school counselor's perspective, covering grades K through 12. She describes the counselor's role in assisting student athletes to "actualize" themselves. This often includes helping them overcome peer pressure, stress and anxiety that might be family related, and other problems that arise as they struggle with their dual roles of student and athlete. The chapter includes a practical guide for school counselors who work with student athletes.

In chapter 3, "Issues in Counseling Athletes at the High School Level," Sara Joy Bailey shares a multifaceted program that she developed and which was successfully implemented in a high school in Memphis, Tennessee. The program was designed to train student athletes to compete both academically and physically at the high school level. The approach is a practical one involving counselors, coaches, faculty, parents, and the athletes themselves. This program can be adopted at other schools.

In chapter 4, "Role Models: An Athlete's Perspective," Dick Barnett reminds the reader of the impact that athletics have on our children, especially at-risk youngsters. The electronic media (television) provides immediate exposure to the athlete, who is then placed, wanted or not, in the position of a role model. The author postulates that several factors contribute to this phenomenon. Such factors include the fact that athletes, unlike some other professional or corporate personages, often have skills that are familiar to the youngsters. Athletes' income levels are also revealed, while corporate income levels remain essentially unknown to the at-risk child. The author, a well-known former athlete, is addressing the issue of role modeling by establishing the Athletic Role Model Education Program. His premise is that every child can learn. The utilization of professional athletes is the key to the success of the approach, which does include cognitive-based activities and state-of-the-art technology.

In chapter 5, "Coaches and Student Athletes," Gary M. Miller addresses specifics in terms of what role the coach plays with the student athlete and with parents. Results from a comprehensive survey indicate the characteristics the student respondents felt were important for a coach to possess. Additionally, the author conducted his own research with coaches and school counselors regarding their respective perceptions of the role of the coach. The results support many of the previous theories.

In chapter 6, "A Guide for College-Bound Athletes," Gary A. Sailes provides a complete guide for college-bound students. The author addresses various issues that a college-bound athlete faces—the recruitment process, the letter of intent, scholarships, admission requirements, and academic eligibility requirements. He also speaks to the myths and realities of graduation rates and dispels the myth of the "dumb jock."

Part II: Athletics and Special Issues

Chapters 7 through 11 address issues that are considered unique to the student athlete. These include the needs of the college athlete, problem solving, career development, stereotyping, and concerns of the African American athlete.

In chapter 7, "Counseling Athletes in Higher Education," Wayne Lanning and Peter Toye address several issues that can be problematic. They discuss areas of impact such as development of a sense of entitlement, peer group difficulties, conditional acceptance, coping with injuries, dealing with coaches, working with nonvolunteer clients, and the dual role of the counselor. Counselors are admonished not to be patronizing or condescending but to respect and counsel the student athlete in the same professional manner shown to all clients.

In chapter 8, "Problem Solving and Decision Making: Life Skills for Student Athletes," J. Scott Hinkle advises that athletes need guidance and training in transferring their sports-related skills to life skills. The underlying assumption is that athletes do in fact engage in problem-solving techniques in their competitive events, and that if they are given appropriate guidance and counseling they will be able to transfer these skills. A case example illustrates, quite vividly, how this transfer can be effectively implemented.

In chapter 9, "Athletics and Career Development: A Research Model," Victoria D. Coleman and Shirl A. Barker share the basis of their research model, "Strategies: A Model of Career Development for Student Athletes." This model, which is currently being utilized at a major research university, consists of six components: introduction and orientation; self-assessment; decision making; educational, occupational, and community information; preparation for work, leisure, and retirement; and research and evaluation. Implications for personal, academic, and career counselors who provide services to student athletes are discussed.

In chapter 10, "The Negative Stereotyping of Student Athletes," Kevin L. Burke addresses several still-prevalent stereotypes—the stereotype of the "dumb jock," along with some stereotypes that continue to oppress female athletes. The author provides appropriate data to refute, and methods to eradicate, some of these stereotypes.

In chapter 11, "The African American Student Athlete," Wyatt D. Kirk and Sarah V. Kirk look at both the history and the current status of African Americans in sports. They discuss specific processes, such as socialization, that are often buttressed by the isolation and racism that affect student athletes and professional athletes. The authors examine several myths that continue to persist regarding the African American athlete, as well as the corresponding reality. They also point out some of the roles of the helping professional as such roles relate to the specific needs of this segment of the population.

Part III: External Forces and the Athlete

Chapters 12 through 15 focus on those forces external to athletes which affect their lives. These forces include the media, the NCAA, sports medicine, and law.

In chapter 12, "The Media's Effect on Athletics," Charles S. Farrell addresses the impact of the media, both electronic and print, on athletics in general and the athlete in particular. He discusses the history of sports writing, the current trends, and the media's portrayal of black athletes and college athletes. Readers are also provided with some practical solutions to the alleged problems.

In chapter 13, "The Role of the NCAA," Wilford S. Bailey describes in a very detailed yet succinct manner the role of the NCAA, and reminds the reader that this organization is a voluntary one, comprised of approximately 800 colleges and universities. Representatives of the colleges and universities adopt and implement all the rules and regulations. The charge to the reader is that those interested in the welfare of the student athlete must continue to work to achieve a balance between academics and athletics.

In chapter 14, "Controversies in Sports Medicine," Karl B. Fields and Martha J. Delaney address myths and realities as they pertain to the following six areas of sports medicine: gender and sport; medical illness and sport; sudden death, cardiac disease, and sport; concussion as a minor risk in sports; anabolic steroid controversies; and psychological factors in injury. Some myths have been largely dispelled, but others still persist. The authors urge their colleagues in sports medicine to continue to provide objective, unemotional advice in a nonjudgmental manner.

In chapter 15, "Law and Sports," George W. Schubert and Arline F. Schubert discuss the many aspects of law and sports. They remind the reader that institutions of higher learning can be sued. Areas such as negligence, due process, gender discrimination, and equal opportunity, as well as drug testing, agents, and the letter of intent, are each reviewed from a legal standpoint. The authors point out the repercussions that can result when certain rules are not adhered to. Such repercussions can affect both the student athlete and the institution.

Finally, case studies and discussion questions are provided that serve to emphasize points discussed throughout the book.

In the Conclusion the Kirks stress the importance of counseling in helping student athletes achieve their developmental and personal goals.

ACKNOWLEDGMENTS

The editors wish to express their deep appreciation to all of the contributors to this book, without whose cooperation this endeavor would not have been possible.

We are indebted to the ACA media committee for their support. We give a special thanks to Elaine Pirrone, ACA Acquisitions and Development Editor, for her critical comments, suggestions, and support.

We wish also to thank Charlayne Gray for her technical aid and assistance in the preparation of the manuscript, and Terri D. Long for her secretarial and computer assistance.

Last, but not least, we extend a special thanks to Dr. John McFadden, who saw the value of such a book, recommended us, and supported and encouraged us as we undertook this project.

CONTRIBUTORS

Editors

Wyatt D. Kirk received his BA, his MS, and his EdD from Western Michigan University. He chairs the Department of Human Development and Services and is an associate professor at North Carolina A&T State University. He is a former high school coach and counselor in Benton Harbor, Michigan, and was a counselor and faculty member at Western Michigan University. His areas of research and specialization include multicultural counseling, research on racism and mental health, and sports psychology. He has published numerous articles and papers on the effects of racism and oppression on identity and self-esteem. He chaired the National Association of Multicultural Counseling, National Division, Symposium on Academics, Athletes, and Black Student Athletes. He is a former member of the editorial board for the *Journal of Multicultural Counseling and Development*, a current member of the editorial board of *Counselor Education and Supervision*, and immediate past chair of the Southern Region Branch Assembly of the American Counseling Association.

Sarah V. Kirk received her BA from St. Augustine's College, her MSW from Atlanta University, and her PhD in social work from the University of Pittsburgh. She is currently chairperson and associate professor in the Department of Sociology and Social Work at North Carolina A&T State University, Greensboro, North Carolina. She has worked as a medical social worker at the University of North Carolina, Chapel Hill, and at Johns Hopkins University Hospital, and as a faculty member at Howard University's School of Social Work, Western Michigan University's School of Social Work, and Virginia Commonwealth University's School of Social Work. Her areas of research and specialization include cultural diversity, women and the "glass ceiling," and issues of self-esteem, and she has published in these areas. She serves as chairperson of the Greensboro Commission on the Status of Women, is a member of Guilford County's Social Services Board, and is cofounder of Greensboro Women Working to Improve Race Relations. She is a member of the National Association of Social Workers, the National Association of Black Social Workers, and the Council on Social Work Education. She was listed in *Who's Who in Black America*, 1990. Dr. Kirk conducts multicultural workshops with her husband, Dr. Wyatt D. Kirk.

Contributors

Sara Jøy Bailey received her BA and MA from Memphis State University and her PhD from the University of Florida. She is a national certified counselor, is certified by the State of Tennessee as a counselor, and has Tennessee teaching credentials. She is a retired counselor from Memphis City Schools and currently is director of the Children's Ministry of Trinity Baptist Church in Southaven, Mississippi. She is past president of both the West Tennessee Association for Counseling and Development and the Tennessee Association for Counseling and Development, and past chairperson of the Southern Region of the American Counseling Association. She has been a presenter at national and state conventions, educational in-service programs, and special interest groups. She is a contributor to the West Tennessee Association for Counseling and Development journal. Her special interest is in developmental counseling programs.

Wilford S. Bailey received his DVM and MS from Auburn University and the SCD from Johns Hopkins University. He is currently a president emeritus and professor at Auburn University. He has 25 years of teaching and research experience and has served for 20 years in academic and scientific administration, including 2 years at the National Institutes of Health. He is the recipient of many awards for professional accomplishments, including Science Faculty Fellow and Scholar in Residence at Rockefellor Foundation International Study and Conference Center, Bellagio, Italy. He is past president of the American Society of Parasitologists, the American Society of Tropical Medicine, and the National Collegiate Athletic Association, and an NCAA senior author of *Athletics and Academe: An Anatomy of Abuses and a Prescription for Reform*. He is currently a consultant for the President's Commission of the NCAA.

Shirl A. Barker is a doctoral student in vocational and technical education at Purdue University. She received a BA in social studies and an MSEd in counseling and development from Purdue University. A licensed professional counselor and a national certified counselor, she is also a research assistant in vocational and technical education. Her research interests are career development and multicultural relations, and she has several publications related to these topics.

Dick Barnett received his BS from California State Poly-technic University, Pomona, his master's from New York University, and his EdD from Fordham University. He is currently president of the Athletic Role Model Education Institute, an adjunct professor at Baruch College, and a sports marketing consultant. His publications include one book and several magazine and newspaper articles. Special interests include writing, lecturing, and using the exposure, persona, charisma, and leadership qualities of professional athletes to influence the cognitive and social development of situational learners. He played 14 years in the NBA, 9 of those years with the New York Knickerbockers as player and assistant coach.

Kevin L. Burke is an assistant professor of sports psychology in the Department of Physical Education at Northern Illinois University. Dr. Burke received his BA from Belmont Abbey College, his MA from East Carolina University, and his PhD from Florida State University. He is a charter member and past executive board member of the Association for the Advancement of Applied Sport Psychology (AAASP). He is also a member of the American Psychological Association and the North American Society for the Psychology of Sport and Physical Activity. He is currently serving as associate editor for the AAASP newsletter and as coeditor for the *Directory of Graduate Programs in Applied Sport Psychology.* He has published many research and popular articles in the field of sports psychology and is currently a Sport Psychologist Digest compiler for the *Journal of Sport and Exercise Psychology.* He has served as a guest reviewer for the *Journal of Applied Sport Psychology, The Sport Psychologist*, and Human Kinetics Publishers. He has served as a member of the research dissemination committee of the Research Consortium of the American Alliance of Health, Physical Education, Recreation and Dance, and as a research works contributing editor for the *Journal of Physical Education, Recreation, and Dance.* His current research interests are in concentration, psychological momentum, humor, burnout, sports officials, and the effectiveness of intervention techniques in sports.

Victoria D. Coleman received an EdD in counseling psychology from Rutgers University. She earned a BA in political science and an MA in U.S. and Latin American history from the University of Iowa, and an MSEd in counselor education from Northern Illinois University. She is a licensed psychologist, a licensed professional counselor, a national certified counselor, and a national certified career counselor. She is currently a counseling psychologist and assistant professor of vocational and technical education at Purdue University. She is also president and owner of The Coleman Group, a management consulting firm in West Lafayette, Indiana, and Detroit, Michigan, specializing in industrial and organizational psychology. Her research interests include career development, multicultural and diverse populations, sports psychology, and entrepreneurship. She has published extensively in these areas.

Martha J. Delaney received both her BA and her MA from the University of North Carolina at Greensboro. She is currently research coordinator at the Family Medicine Residency Program of the Moses H. Cone Memorial Hospital and the Greensboro Area Health Education Center, Greensboro, North Carolina. Her research and publications include articles in *Clinical Sports Medicine* and the *Journal of Family Practice.* Her special interests are sports medicine, substance abuse, and clinical services.

Charles S. Farrell, a career journalist, is president of Sports Perspectives International, an athletes' advocacy organization, and former special projects coordinator for the Center for the Study of Sports in Society at Northeastern University. A graduate of Lincoln University in Pennsylvania, with an MS in journalism from Northwestern University, Farrell became a well-known writer in the area of college sports after he joined the staff of the *Chronicle of Higher Education* in Washington, DC, in 1982. His investigative reporting with the *Chronicle* led to his receiving the Northeastern University Award for Excellence in Sports Journalism for 1986–87. Mr. Farrell joined the *Washington Post* sports department in 1988 as a writer and editor, positions he held until joining the Center for the Study of Sports in Society in August, 1989. As president of Sports Perspectives International, which he founded in 1988, Mr. Farrell coproduced the first, second, and third annual Black Athletes in America forums in 1989, 1990, and 1991. Mr. Farrell is also a contributing author of *The Rules of the Game: Ethics in College Sports*.

Karl B. Fields received his BA from Yale University and his MD from the University of Kentucky School of Medicine. He is associate director of the Family Medicine Residency Program of the Moses H. Cone Memorial Hospital, Greensboro, North Carolina. He has published in the *Journal of Family Practice*, *The Physician and Sports Medicine*, and *Essentials of Family Medicine*.

Mary Mitchell Harris received her PhD and her MS in social psychology from the University of Pittsburgh and her BS in psychology from Duke University. She is founder and president of Harris Learning Systems, Inc., and performance counselor at Georgia Tech Athletic Association in Atlanta, Georgia. She is also former president of the Association of Black Psychologists, Atlanta Chapter, and former president of the Mental Health Association of Metropolitan Atlanta. Her research and publications include the self-published work *Is Your Child Ok? Transactional Analysis for the Public Classroom*, *Coping With Stress and Ego Involvement in Blood Pressure Control*, *A Transactional Analysis of the Black Experience*, *Predicting the Null in Women's Research With Black Populations*, *Do Black Women Need Achievement?*, and *Power Learning: A Game Plan for Student Athletes*.

J. Scott Hinkle received his PhD from Florida State University. He is an assistant professor at the University of North Carolina-Greensboro, where he coordinates the Community Counseling Program and specialty training in sports counseling. He serves on the editorial boards of the *Journal of Mental Health Counseling* and the *Journal of Counseling & Development*, as editor-elect of *The Family Journal*, and as a board member of the International Association of Marriage and Family Counselors. His interests include running, cycling, the triathlon, and white water kayaking.

Wayne Lanning received his BA from Calvin College, his MA from Michigan State University, and his EdD from Western Michigan University. He is professor and chair of the Department of Counseling and Educational Psychology at the University of Nevada, Las Vegas. He has authored a number of publications in counseling and sports psychology, including a chapter in a sports psychology book. He originated and developed Northern Rocky Mountain Educational Research Associations. He has engaged in extensive consultations in sports psychology including the U.S. Olympic men's track and field athletes and coaches, Indiana University basketball, and the University of Wyoming basketball teams. He is a licensed professional counselor in Wyoming and a licensed counseling psychologist in Indiana. Among his special interests are ethics and professional practices, development of counselor education programs, and counseling supervision.

Gary M. Miller received his BS from Slippery Rock State College, his MEd from Duquesne University, a Certificate of Advanced Studies from Kent State University, and a PhD from Case Western Reserve University. He is associate professor at the College of Education at the University of South Carolina, a nationally certified counselor, a licensed professional counselor in South Carolina, a licensed professional counselor supervisor in South Carolina, and a licensed counseling psychologist in South Carolina. He has published in many of the journals of the American Counseling Association. He has coedited books and monographs and has coauthored the book *The Middle School Counselor*. He has developed a course focusing on the systematic training of counselors, and he recently developed the course "Counseling Student Athletes," which is designed for counselors, coaches, and athletic directors in elementary and secondary schools. At the national level, he has developed a special interest network in the American School Counselor Association (ASCA) focusing on the counseling and development of student athletes.

Beverly J. O'Bryant is the Executive Assistant to the Superintendent of the District of Columbia Public Schools for the Office of Parental Involvement and Community Support. She is president of Counseling and Training Systems, Inc., and a former counselor with the District of Columbia Public Schools, having worked at the elementary, middle/junior, and senior high school levels. She is immediate past president of the 15,000-member American School Counselor Association, and president-elect of the American Counseling Association. She has also served as an adjunct professor at Mississippi State University. Mrs. O'Bryant received her BA in elementary education from Dunbarton College and an MA in counseling from the University of Maryland. She is currently a doctoral student at Nova University in Florida. She is a nationally certified counselor as well as a nationally certified school counselor. She is the recipient of numerous awards and honors, including Exemplary Leadership Resolutions from the District of Columbia City Council and the School Board of the District of Columbia, and a government relations award for outstanding legislative lobbying from the American Counseling Association.

Gary A. Sailes received his PhD from the University of Minnesota. He is an assistant professor of sports psychology at Indiana University. He is founder and director of the Indiana Sports and Education Foundation. Dr. Sailes has written and lectured extensively about intercollegiate sports, and has published in several research journals. He is currently engaged in funded research to determine the academic accountability of intercollegiate athletics.

Arline F. Schubert received her BS in English education from the University of North Dakota and the JD, also from the University of North Dakota. She is currently serving as legal counselor and as an English instructor at the University of North Dakota. She is a member of the American Bar Association and of the State of North Dakota Bar Association, and is licensed to practice law in North Dakota and in the federal court in the District of North Dakota. She has published articles in two law review journals—the *North Dakota Law Review* and the *Seton Hall Journal of Sports Law*—and has authored numerous articles on sports law and on advising student athletes. She has also presented papers at two international conferences.

George W. Schubert received his BS from the University of Wisconsin, La Crosse, his MS from the University of Wisconsin, Madison, and his PhD from the University of Washington, Seattle. At the University of North Dakota, he acts as Dean of the University College and Summer Sessions, professor of communication disorders, and faculty athletic representative. He has authored or coauthored four books and approximately 50 articles, coauthored one book supplement, and presented 62 papers, including international, national, regional, and state presentations. He is a Fellow of the American Speech-Language-Hearing Association and holds a certificate of clinical competence in speech pathology. He received the Maurice O. Graff Distinguished Alumnus Award from the University of Wisconsin, La Crosse, in 1990.

Peter Toye received his BA from Millersville State College and his MS and PhD from the University of Wyoming. He is Assistant Director of Athletics for Student Services at the University of Wyoming. He serves as chair of the National Association of Academic Advisors for Athletics Research Commission. He is a licensed professional counselor. His special interests are hiking, fishing, writing, and family activities.

INTRODUCTION

Student Athletes: Shattering the Myths and Sharing the Realities

WYATT D. KIRK AND SARAH V. KIRK

> College sport has grown into an expensive circus, driven by an insatiable appetite for winning, and amateur athletes are getting neither the moral guidance nor the education they bargained for. (Sanoff & Schrof, 1990, p. 50)

College sports is being undermined by such issues as public mistrust, mandatory disclosure of graduation rates, and the ongoing debate of college athletics versus professional sports. Many sports enthusiasts believe that the amateur is nonexistent. Additionally, racial stereotyping and the accusations of widespread exploitation are bases for reform, since these issues are not just serious, but systemic.

Largely as a result of the articles, books, and media attention devoted to intercollegiate athletics, many now believe it is time to redefine the role of athletics in higher education. Interestingly, the situation is not a new one. In 1905, President Theodore Roosevelt called university representatives to the White House and cautioned that unless they took action to reduce injuries to players in intercollegiate football games, he would do so by executive decree. In 1929, the Carnegie Foundation examined the problem of college sports in a comprehensive published report called "American College Athletics." The Foundation reached the following conclusion:

> More than any other force, [athletics has] tended to distort the values of college life and to increase its emphasis upon the material and the monetary. Indeed, at no point in the educational process has commercialism

of college athletics wrought more mischief than in its effect upon the
American undergraduate. And the distressing fact is that the college, the
fostering mother, has permitted and even encouraged it to do these
things in the name of education. (Lapchick & Slaughter, 1989)

Today, while the times are different, the circumstances and events
remain the same in many respects. In response to the rising level of concern
the Knight Foundation's Commission was organized.

. . . the Knight Commission was a group of twenty-two leaders from
higher education, business, the Congress, sports and boards of trust-
ees. The Commission's purpose, through hearings and recommendations is to correct abuse in intercollegiate sports and to serve as a
positive influence in retaining intercollegiate sports programs.
("Knight Commission Report," March 1990, p. A38)

In a 47-page report, this commission, in March 1991, echoed some of the
same concerns pointed out earlier, and presented 30 recommendations designed to restore integrity and public confidence in intercollegiate sports
and the sponsoring universities. As a result of this report and others during
the past 10 years, a new concern has surfaced, that being the overall welfare
of student athletes. Many groups want "student" put back in "student athlete." One such group is made up of the professionals in the mental health
field, particularly counselors and sports psychologists, whose involvement
has increased over the past decade.

Such programs continue to be needed but are limited. Numerous other
articles (Goldberg, 1991; Lanning, 1982; Petitpas & Champagne, 1988; Wittmer, Bostic, Phillips, & Waters, 1981) have echoed the same message, citing
the need of student athletes for professional assistance with academic, athletic, and psychosocial problems. Specifically, student athletes may need
counseling to help them cope with success or the lack of success, identity
conflict, social isolation, exploitation, alcohol and drugs, stress and burnout,
poor athletic performance, academic and vocational concerns, and transition
and retirement concerns. Chartrand and Lent (1987) have suggested a research agenda to deal with the aforementioned concerns.

The Association for Counselor Education and Supervision (Hinkle,
1989) broadly defines sports counseling as a helping process that incorporates
education and treatment. Education refers to preventive programs and developing self-concepts, while treatment refers to interventions concerning
life-style consultation, developmental problems, program organization and
evaluation, maximizing performance, competitive stress reduction, and clinical problems. Counselors and athletes alike should know and understand
the role of both education and treatment.

Schubert and Gilbert (1986) define counselor roles as follows: they
need to accept that the student athlete is assisting the institution by dis-
playing athletic skills and the institution is assisting the student athlete by
providing an educational opportunity. Schubert and Gilbert suggest that

student athletes, through their athletic experience, need to learn about courage, leadership, self-expectation, discipline, pride, sacrifice, ethics, failure, and success. The optimal goal is to create an environment in which the student athlete will assimilate experiences and formal education, thereby becoming an asset to his or her profession and to society.

MYTHS AND REALITIES

Myth and reality might be considered oxymorons, because they often contradict each other in meaning. A myth is for all an inverted story, a tale of imagined persons or events. The idea is akin to that of a fable or even a fairy tale (Reik, 1970). Conversely, reality is the quality or fact of being real, or the property of being true to life. Unfortunately, many of the problems encountered in working with athletes are products not only of how they are seen by themselves and others, but also of what they themselves fail to see (Remer, Tongate, & Watson, 1978). In other words, when athletes choose myths as a source, they are putting their faith in something other than themselves. With athletics, myths are dreams that collide with reality. This book will bring forth many such myths and the attending realities.

DEFINITION OF TERMS

It is necessary and appropriate that at this juncture we define terms, rules, and athletics facts that are referred to throughout this book.

- **Proposition 48** refers to Division I colleges and universities requiring their incoming freshmen to attain a minimum score of 700 on the Scholastic Aptitude Test (SAT), or 15 on the American College Testing Program's Standardized Test, and a 2.0 grade point average in 11 high school core courses to be eligible to play intercollegiate sports their first year (Bailey & Littleton, 1991).
- **Revenue-producing sports** are those which reputedly bring large sums of money to Division I schools. For the purpose of this book, those sports are football, baseball, basketball (both men's and women's), hockey, and soccer in selected institutions.
- **Graduation rates** (released by the NCAA) which are appropriate for this book and included in several chapters indicate that only 26.6% of African American student athletes graduate, compared to 52.2% of Whites, and that 45.7% of all athletes graduate.
- **Proposition 16**, which was officially passed at the recent annual NCAA meeting in Anaheim, California, is included for information only. It is not effective until 1995, and is subject to revisions prior to implementation. Essentially, it would require freshman athletes to have a 2.5 grade point average in a core curriculum of 13 high school courses. There may be some variations based on indexing.

- **Minority athletes** refers to African American student athletes or professionals. The term is so defined because there are a limited number of other minority student athletes involved in intercollegiate athletics (particularly revenue-producing sports) and in professional sports.

CONCLUSION

The problems in athletics are not insurmountable, but in the future we must create new programs of support and assistance for student athletes as well as take full advantage of those already in place. Holistic support programs that address psychosocial issues in academics and athletics can provide necessary assistance to student athletes, through intervention and strategies that view the athlete as an individual with changing needs and skills, rather than exclusively as an athletic participant. Because student athletes are a unique population, the process must include both education and treatment—the areas that are presented in this book.

References

Bailey, W. S., & Littleton, T. D. (1991). *Athletics and academe: An anatomy of abuses and a prescription for reform.* New York: Macmillan.

Chartrand, J. M., & Lent, R. W. (1987). Sports counseling: Enhancing the development of the athlete. *Journal of Counseling and Development, 66,* 164–167.

Goldberg, A. D. (1991). Counseling the high school student athlete. *The School Counselor, 38,* 332–339.

Hinkle, S. (1989, Fall). ACES sports counseling interest network formed. *ACES Spectrum, 50*(1), 10.

Knight Commission report. (1990, March 7). *Chronicle of Higher Education,* p. A38.

Lanning, W. (1982). The privileged few: Special counseling needs of athletes. *Journal of Sport Psychology, 4,* 19–23.

Lapchick, K. E., & Slaughter, J. B. (1989). *The rules of the game: Ethics in college sports.* New York: Macmillan.

Petitpas, A. J., & Champagne, D. E. (1988). Developmental programming for intercollegiate athletes. *Journal of College Student Development, 29*(5), 454–460.

Reik, T. (1970). *Myth and guilt.* New York: Grosset and Dunlap.

Remer, R., Tongate, R. A., & Watson, J. (1978). Athletes: Counseling the overprivileged minority. *The Personnel and Guidance Journal, 56,* 616–629.

Sanoff, A. P., & Schrof, J. M. (1990, January 8). The price of victory. *U.S. News & World Report,* p. 50.

Schubert, G. W., & Gilbert, J. W. (1986). The student-athlete's predicted monetary value to an institution. *The Academic Athletic Journal,* 43–46.

Wittmer, J., Bostic, D., Phillips, T. D., & Waters, W. (1981). The personal, academic, and career problems of college student athletes: Some possible answers. *The Personnel and Guidance Journal, 60,* 52–55.

PART I

THE ATHLETIC ENVIRONMENT

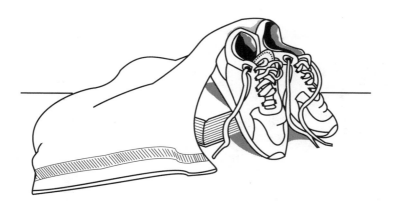

CHAPTER 1

Developmental Benefits of Athletics

MARY MITCHELL HARRIS

Although the benefits to society may be numerous and seldom disputed, the effect of athletic participation on athletes is open to question. The career athlete usually spends a lifetime training, practicing, and participating in the sport. Personal growth dimensions are thought to be influenced in definite ways, perhaps to the detriment of the athlete. For example, myths regarding the athlete's intellect are pervasive in society. The purpose of this chapter is to explore the benefits and risks associated with sport participation for young athletes along developmental lines.

The chapter will address issues regarding the influence of athletic participation during three periods of development—the little league years, the high school years, and the college years. The discussion will be guided by well-known theories of development, including Erikson's social development theory, Chickering's theory of developmental tasks for college students, Piaget's cognitive theory, and Kohlberg's moral development theory. We will conclude with a performance enhancement theory, which predicts potential benefits of athletic participation in the future.

DEVELOPMENTAL THEORIES AND ISSUES IN ATHLETICS

The Psychosocial Development of Athletes

Erik Erikson's theory of psychosocial development holds that the healthy personality is the consequence of an individual's successfully negotiating predictable issues at certain stages of life. Eight successive stages are presented, which cover the entire human life span. The stages that are pertinent to our discussion are:

- Stage 4: Industry versus inferiority (Ages 6 through 12), and
- Stage 5: Identity versus identity diffusion and role confusion (Ages 12 through 18) (Shaffer, 1985).

Industry versus inferiority and the little league years. According to Erikson, school-age youngsters compare themselves to peers to determine who they are and what they are capable of. If they achieve the major goals of this period, which include acquiring both academic and social skills, children at this stage will develop a sense of industry and self-esteem (Shaffer, 1985).

Little league sport participation is an ideal social structure to facilitate the development of industry. Making the team when others are cut, and emerging as a consistent, dependable player, provide the occasion for developing competence and industry. Crucial social skills like cooperation and fair play are easily forged. The little leaguer can also sense the importance of successful performance to adults, namely the coaches and parents. Peer approval and adult recognition are easily won through sport participation.

Determining identity through athletics. As children become adolescents, the determinants of self-esteem will change. The many physical, social, and emotional changes that occur at puberty force them to reevaluate themselves and their goals in search of a stable identity (Shaffer, 1985). Identity, or the sense of oneself, is achieved when appropriate social roles are integrated, leading to marriage and adult occupation (Lyons & Barrell, 1979).

Increasingly, time spent in the sport and accolades received for successful performance will forge a personal identity around athletics. The media announce sports accomplishments, shaping an important role for athletes in the community. Successful athletes leave high school with a strong sense of self and clear goals for pursuing a professional career during the college years. Erikson's theory predicts that adolescents who do not develop a strong sense of self will enter adulthood with considerable role confusion or identity diffusion. It is not likely that the athlete will experience such a crisis.

Pros and cons. On the surface, the influence of athletic participation on psychosocial development appears to be decidedly advantageous. Competence, industry, and role identity seem to follow naturally from successful sport participation. Risks do exist, however, especially at the high school level. The influence of the media and the spectator following may fix identity and establish a career role prematurely. Recent investigators have shown that people go through several phases before establishing a stable self-concept. High school is perhaps too early to forge a firm, future-oriented self-image, which has been shown to develop through a gradual and somewhat uneven process (Whittemore, 1985). The influence of athletic participation on psychosocial development seems beneficial overall, but must be qualified along the line just discussed.

Developmental Tasks for College Athletes

The rites of passage of collegiate athletes into adulthood and maturity are the same as those for other young adults. Chickering (1969), a major contributor to this area, has identified three developmental tasks appropriate for college students, which are described as follows:

- Task I: Developing autonomy. *Subtasks*: instrumental and emotional autonomy, interdependence.
- Task II: Developing mature interpersonal relationships. *Subtasks*: tolerance, relationships with peers and with members of the opposite sex.
- Task III: Developing purpose. *Subtasks*: appropriate educational plans, career plans, life-style plans.

Student athletes, like all freshmen, face these same issues and tasks. Their uniquely different college life experiences have an impact on the accomplishment of these tasks.

Developing autonomy. For the college athlete, gaining emotional independence from parents is replaced with gaining emotional independence from the coach. At many institutions, the athletic department determines most of the academic and student life decisions for the student athlete. As a consequence, many athletes do not develop the social skills necessary to successfully negotiate campus life. They feel uncomfortable approaching a typical university situation, and usually are characterized as irresponsible for leaving things undone (Whittemore, 1985). While the typical college student's development of emotional and instrumental autonomy is aided by the physical distance separating the student from his or her parents, the collegiate athlete is thrown into a tighter web with adults, namely coaches and academic staff members. Rigid structure around meetings, training, practice, and study times leaves little emotional or physical space to develop autonomy.

Nevertheless, the successful student athlete is distinguished in remarkable ways along developmental lines, and there are numerous examples. At the author's institution, athletes report that they either register themselves or largely influence their own registration. They consult with advisors about handling conflicts that occur and, within the bounds of athletic and school policy, solve their own problems. They also form interdependencies with other students which expand their experience of success both in the classroom and in campus life.

Developing mature interpersonal relations. Developing tolerance means that the young adult learns to accept others for their merits rather than judge them on the basis of ethnic background, personal appearance, or first impressions (Chickering, 1969). Collegiate athletics provides a unique opportunity for developing tolerance, since most Division I teams are made up of a racially diverse group of players who live, work, study, practice, travel, and play together. They esteem each other based largely on merit and decided accomplishments in the sport.

Completion of the interpersonal relations task is hampered, however, by time constraints, athletic housing, and training tables, which segregate the athlete from nonathlete peers. Isolation was the single most reported complaint of Black student athletes who responded to a survey conducted by the National Collegiate Athletic Association ("Research Institute," 1989). The separation of athletes from nonathletes on campus contributes to suspiciousness, unrealistic expectations, negative perceptions, and stereotypes. The nonathlete's attitude may vacillate between hero worship on the one hand and anger or jealousy on the other, in response to rumors of preferential treatment. Peers may expect and therefore reinforce stereotypic "jock" attitudes and narrow social skills among athletes (Whittemore, 1985). These attitudes push student athletes into further isolation, where their only real friends are other athletes.

Black and female athletes face additional issues. Some Black athletes have expressed concern that athletics is just another form of servitude (Green, Gunnings, & McMillan, 1972). Female athletes might encounter negative stigma, particularly if they compete in the "masculine sports," like basketball. Some people believe that a possible outcome of sport competition is the loss of femininity, and that the female participant is actually masculinized not just physically but also psychologically and behaviorally (Anthrop & Allison, 1983). Race and gender appear to complicate the task of establishing mature peer and heterosexual relations.

Developing purpose. Purpose is achieved through the execution of a meaningful educational plan connected to realistic career plans (Chickering, 1969). In no other area is criticism more severe regarding the negative influences of athletics, particularly for Black athletes. Athletic departments have been cited for willfully impeding the normal academic progress of student athletes. Stories about courses in "basket weaving" and majors in "eligibility" are rampant. Contrary to prevalent myths, Black and non-Black athletes in revenue-producing sports tend to place about the same emphasis on the importance of obtaining a college degree. Also, the most popular choice of a major for both groups is business; few major in physical education ("Research Institute," 1989). In terms of life-style goals, Black student athletes place a higher value on career success, job security, financial success, happiness, health, and marriage than do non-Black athletes or Black nonathletes.

Where Black student athletes differ most from other comparison groups is in the area of career aspirations. More than 40% expect to become professional athletes, compared to 20% of their non-Black teammates. In reality, fewer than 5% actually become professionals ("Research Institute," 1989). College involvement definitely influences unrealistic expectations about professional careers.

Myths About Intellectual Development

Origin of the myth. For centuries philosophers debated the relationship between the mind and the body. Men in the 19th century argued that the mind was separate from the body, and felt that a strong body and a bright mind could not coexist. This position was revived by psychologists in the 1950s to explain the unexpected findings that showed that African babies were far ahead of European babies in psychomotor development (Geber, 1958). Afraid of the implications of such findings, psychologists interpreted the findings as indicating that body functions were separate from mental attributes. Such interpretations sought to limit the African infant's advanced status to physical qualities alone. The "all brawn, no brain" myth appears to have its origin not in science but in the biased conclusions of European thought.

The brain and belief. Myths about the intelligence of athletes are pervasive, and have a direct though subtle effect upon the development of intellect. To the extent that athletes themselves internalize negative beliefs about their intelligence, myths become reality for them. Beliefs are acted on by the subconscious mind through the reticular activating system (RAS) of the brain (Harris, 1988). The perceptual function of the RAS is to bring to the attention all the evidence in one's environment which validates the beliefs held about oneself and the world. Information inconsistent with those beliefs goes unnoticed (Harris, 1988). The brain subsequently shapes behavior to bring about the object of the belief. This may translate into not being able to stay awake in class, carelessly misreading test items, drawing blanks, or showing up at the wrong time or place for a test.

Involvement in athletics does not impede the progression of the young person through the stages of cognitive development described by Piaget. However, deep psychological processes and cognitive structures are sensitive to prevalent beliefs about the student athlete's intellectual potential. Myth becomes reality if the student athlete internalizes these beliefs.

Current Issues Concerning the Moral Development of Athletes

"Can Athletes Learn Not to Cheat?" was a title that created alarm at a recent workshop on moral reasoning in athletes (Beller & Stoll, 1991). Soon after, another shocking title surfaced—"See Dick and Jane Lie, Cheat and Steal" (Fleisher, 1991). What initially registered as an ethical shortcoming among athletes appears actually to be pervasive among the general student population.

The Stoll and Beller (1991) research project was designed to test the hypothesis that "university age athletes are less reasoned and less developed morally than their university age peers" (p. 3). The result of a cross-cultural study of university-age athletes from this country and Korea supported the hypothesis. Using a newly constructed instrument called the Hahm-Beller Values Choice Inventory in the Sport Milieu and the Defining Issues Test, a recognized instrument for measuring moral development, the researchers found that "male athletes were morally developed at about a sixth–seventh grade level while their peer groups were developed at about the fourteenth grade level. Female athletes were developed at about a ninth–tenth grade level while their peer group was developed at about a twelfth to thirteenth grade level" (Stoll & Beller, 1991, p. 4).

According to Kohlberg's theory of moral development, these findings suggest that student athletes are a stage and a half behind their peers. Sixth-graders base their moral judgment of a situation on the consequences of an act, while morality for the college-age student is based on the desire to comply with formal laws and customs to maintain good relationships. Some might infer that participation in sport in some way interferes with moral development.

Before they can reasonably conclude that sport involvement does interfere with moral development, researchers will need to consider and refute a number of alternative hypotheses. For example, research has shown that athletes have a strong right-brain orientation (Wonder & Donovan, 1984). Reasoning ability is a left-brain function. The moral reasoning tests may be distinguishing athletes from their peers based more on cognitive style preference than on moral deficiency. When it comes to drawing inferences from research around ethical issues, caution is advised.

The Stoll and Beller (1991) project also features a successful intervention course in moral reasoning for student athletes. Courses in ethics are also being developed for business majors, engineering majors, and medical students. Ethical issues in society are pervasive, and remedies need to be addressed in a variety of ways. Selecting out student athletes as a special case will not serve a meaningful purpose, and will only give rise to new stereotypes.

POTENTIAL BENEFITS OF SPORT PARTICIPATION FROM A NEW AGE PERSPECTIVE

The Wholistic[1] View

A wholistic view of humankind was reflected in the ancient Greeks' belief that inside every strong body was a sound mind. Today education is going full circle to incorporate this original notion in a new education paradigm

---

[1]Author's preferred spelling.

which features wholism (Schwartz, 1984). Whole-brain, or left-brain/right-brain, education takes advantage of new information about how the brain is organized to conduct life activities. The left side of the brain is responsible for academic skills such as grammar rules, sequential thinking, and analytical ability. The right brain conducts creative activities such as art, music, rhythm, imagination, and body awareness.

Athletes and brain dominance. Athletes have shown a strong right-brain orientation (Wonder & Donovan, 1984), which accounts for their execution of skills involving rhythm, timing, and body awareness. Traditional education, however, emphasizes left-brain education and neglects the right side. Students with a right-brain preference are probably not served as well by educators as are left-brain individuals. As a result, many students turn to athletics as a viable channel for exercising their preference for right-brain activities (Harris, 1988).

Wholistic education is predicted to replace old paradigms in the future, and, as described, it will be an education for "right-brain development— education through the arts and the senses and the feelings" (Schwartz, 1984, p. 2). Student athletes will have a distinct advantage in that teaching styles will target their cognitive preference.

Performance Enhancement Theory

A companion theory also predicts that the student athlete will benefit greatly in the future. Sport psychology has built a tradition for examining the psychological factors in athletic competition (Nideffer, 1976). Initially, much was learned by simply asking world-class athletes how they mentally prepared for the game (Kriegel & Kriegel, 1984). Consistently, athletes reported engaging positive self-talk, running mental movies of successful plays, and amplifying positive affect around the anticipation of winning. Performance enhancement theory emerged from these reports as a science for understanding how to forge human qualities to generate excellence in all areas of life. As a result, performance enhancement training is now used by a wide variety of professional groups—for example, business, sales, and the performing arts (Kriegel & Kriegel, 1984).

Power Learning Theory

Most recently, these same principles were incorporated into a program of academic support for the student athlete (Harris, 1988). Research engaged initially to promote performance in the game now serves as a base for supporting the student athlete in the classroom. Power learning theory predicts that athletes can use themselves as models to generate personal success in academics. Student athletes learn much from their sport, and power learning helps them reframe this learning for classroom success. This cognitive reframing process reveals the mental skills that account for their success in the sport, and draws parallels to be practiced for the classroom.

For example, the mind-body centering process that the athlete engages spontaneously to create readiness for a play is applied to create readiness for study or test taking. The student athlete is asked to report on the stylized way that a free-throw shooter, or a golfer, bowler, or batter, prepares for a shot. He is told to notice that each athlete has a unique method of preparation but that they all have something in common—the breath taken at the end which sets the response. The student athlete is then taught a simple centering exercise that involves breathing and visualization. The centering process should be engaged in preparation for study, test taking, oral reports, and other academic activities.

Power learning programs are being introduced to student athletes both in school systems and in the community. The aim of the program creator is to participate in the shaping of a new paradigm for educating athletes, one which will focus on the development of the total person. The future holds definite benefits for those who choose to participate in sports.

CONCLUSION

From a developmental perspective, participation in sports has both its benefits and its risks. Athletics contributes to psychosocial development in youth by facilitating the acquisition of social skills and industry. Identity is easily forged during adolescence through athletic participation. Identity and career choice may be shaped prematurely, however, before the young person has sufficiently sampled interests and talents. The conclusion that psychosocial development through adolescence is aided by sport participation is reached with this caution in mind.

Participation at the college level reveals more risks than benefits. The development of autonomy is threatened by the rigidly structured life of college athletes. As a consequence, some do not develop necessary social skills and appear irresponsible. This contributes to "jock attitude" stereotypes held by the community. Although college athletics provides a great opportunity to develop tolerance, especially around ethnic and racial issues, it hampers the expansion of friendships with nonathlete peers. Isolation limits the athlete's opportunity to develop mature interpersonal relationships. Black and female athletes encounter additional prejudices from peers.

The role athletics plays in developing purpose has come under harsh criticism. Contrary to prevalent rumors, athletes choose meaningful majors, place a high value on obtaining a degree, and have life-style goals similar to those of nonathletes.

The old myth about the athlete's inferior intellectual ability may be traced to its probable origin in the biased interpretation of research that separated the mind from body functions. The effect of beliefs on brain structures can explain why some athletes act out the myth. The effects of such internalization of myths aside, cognitive development is believed to proceed along its course with athletes much as it does with the typical student.

Joining old myths may be a new one concerning the moral development of athletes. Recent findings show that college athletes "lag behind" in moral reasoning. A much better purpose is served if athletes are regarded as just one of a number of groups who might benefit from ethics courses.

Proponents of athletic participation can look to the future with optimism. The move toward wholism is mandating a new educational paradigm to develop the right brain, for which athletes have shown a preference. Performance enhancement principles, derived from the successes of athletes, are now being used to promote performance in many areas of life. One immediate application is being made in academics with the power learning model. Power learning uses sport psychology techniques to promote learning in the classroom. Today's student athlete and those of the future stand to benefit greatly from new perspectives in education.

References

Anthrop, J., & Allison, M. (1983). Role conflict and the high school female athlete. *Research Quarterly for Exercise and Sport, 54*, 104–11.

Beller, J., & Stoll, S. (1991, June). *Morality and sport: Can athletes learn not to cheat? A moral reasoning intervention program for Division I athletes.* Paper presented at the meeting of the National Association for Academic Advisors for Athletes, Atlanta, GA.

Chickering, A. (1969). *Education and identity.* San Francisco: Jossey-Bass.

Fleisher, C. (Producer/Director). (1991). *See Dick and Jane lie, cheat and steal: Teaching morality to kids.* [Videotape]. Santa Monica, CA: Pyramid Film and Video.

Geber, M. (1958). The psychomotor development of African children in the first year. *Journal of Social Psychology, 47*, 185–195.

Green, P., Gunnings, T., & McMillan, J. (1972). The status of Blacks in the Big Ten: Issues and concerns. *Journal of Non-White Concerns in Personnel and Guidance, 3*, 28–38.

Harris, M. (1988). *Power learning: A game plan for student athletes and other active learners.* Atlanta: Harris Learning Systems, Inc.

Kriegel, R., & Kriegel, M. (1984). *The C zone: Peak performance under pressure.* Garden City, NY: Anchor Press/Doubleday.

Lyons, J., & Barrell, J. (1979). *People: An introduction to psychology.* New York: Harper and Row.

Nideffer, R. (1976). *The inner athlete.* San Diego: Enhanced Performance Associates.

Research institute releases study of Black student-athletes. (1989, Sept.). *National Collegiate Athletic Association News, 25*, p. 1.

Schwartz, R. (1984, March). Whole brain education. *The Tarrytown Letter*, p. 2.

Shaffer, D. (1985). *Developmental psychology.* Belmont, CA: Wadsworth.

Stoll, S., & Beller, J. (1991, June). *The University of Idaho, Institute for Ethics.* Handout given with presentation at the National Association for Academic Advisors for Athletes, Atlanta, GA.

Whittemore, W. (1985, Fall). The college student athlete: Special needs and development inventions. *The National Advisor.*

Wonder, J., & Donovan, P. (1984). *Whole brain thinking.* New York: William Morrow.

CHAPTER 2

School Counseling and the Student Athlete

BEVERLY J. O'BRYANT

THE SCHOOL COUNSELOR AND THE COMPREHENSIVE DEVELOPMENTAL COUNSELING PROGRAM

The school counselor is a certified professional educator who assists students, teachers, parents, and administrators. School counselors work with all students to help develop their educational, social, career, and personal strengths so that they will become responsible, productive citizens. School counseling programs are comprehensive and developmental by design, focusing on needs, interests, and issues related to the various stages of student growth (American School Counselor Association [ASCA], 1990). A developmental school counseling program should be implemented in every school, prekindergarten through postsecondary, and should emphasize and capitalize on prevention and the acquisition of life skills in lieu of constant remediation and crisis intervention.

THE MYTHS AND REALITIES ABOUT STUDENT ATHLETES

Young minds are not necessarily grounded in reality, and very often it is adult intervention that helps to perpetuate myth and distort reality. Human nature seems to dictate that each generation strive to surpass the one preceding it. This theory, carried to its logical conclusion, seems to necessitate that child surpass parent, that succeeding cultures and mores advance, and that generations advance technologically in significant increments. The logical consequences of this thinking, however, are the intertwining of mythical and realistic precepts, the processing, analyzing, and conceptualizing of strategies to respond to those "real/myth" precepts, and the eventual institutionalization of a "real/myth" as a reality-based concept.

Student Perceptions

Students begin such sports as tee ball, soccer, football, and gymnastics in organized leagues at 5 and 6 years of age, before they have developed emotionally or physically and before they have even the slightest concept of a direction for life. At this age, developmentally, children's positive self-regard is almost directly proportionate to their abilities to please their parents and/or significant others in their lives. Conversely, those significant others spend significant amounts of time praising the child for the most menial accomplishments, understanding the child's need for success and self-confidence. By preadolescence, the children may perceive themselves as exceptional whether they are or not. They have been exposed to the perceived glamour of the professional athlete, the excitement and thrill of participation in noncompetitive sports, and the apparent monetary and societal gains to be made. They have experienced the personal, social, and emotional rewards realized by participation, and know the satisfaction of pleasing the significant others in their lives. By adolescence, competitive sports can represent a range of experiences from fright to fortune and everything in between. But the constants remain constant: the need to please the significant others in one's life, the need for social acceptance, and the desire to take a perceived "sure-shot" opportunity to achieve the "wants" in life in a potentially lucrative, glamorous fashion.

Adult Perceptions

Adult perceptions, on the other hand, might be quite different from the child's. When the child is 5 or 6 years old, the adult wants the child to experience and be exposed to a myriad of things. The parent does not want the neighbor's or best friend's child to outdo his or her own child. The adult finds sports an acceptable, fun way of being involved with the child, and might subconsciously hope that within that child lies real talent worthy of being nurtured. When the child reaches preadolescence, the adult tends to nurture the child along by offering advice, praising at the appropriate times, and generally corroborating by action or articulation that sports is a definite option for the child and one that would make the parents happy, provide financial security in the future, and provide the social acceptance that would please everyone. By adolescence and early adulthood, the media hype, attention, and privileges afforded professional athletes, and the success and esteem experienced by the student athlete thus far, generally have significantly influenced the student athlete's academic and career decision processes. At this point, student athletes have received so many messages that they are looking to the most significant adults in their lives to assist with critical, sound decision making.

Perpetuation and Institutionalization of Myths

Myths are not only perpetuated by students and adults alike, but have indeed become institutionalized within the social, economic, and psychological structures of the society at large. Sports represent the "pie in the sky" dreams that seem reachable because enough superstar role models exist to attest that they are not impossible dreams. Sports represents a vicarious life for adults, a way to a better existence for the underprivileged, a fulfillment of sustained glory and glamour for those who might already have experienced glamour, and potential security, fame, and fortune for all who choose to associate with sports. The successes experienced by student athletes are all too often "transformed into dreams of recurring glory and career in professional sport" (Landers, Feltz, Obermeier, & Brouse, 1978).

The Cold Hard Facts of Reality

But the realities must also be perpetuated, and the realities also warrant institutionalization. According to the National Collegiate Athletic Association (NCAA, 1990), there are approximately 150,000 seniors among the 525,000 high school students playing interscholastic basketball each year, and about 12,000 collegiate basketball players. Apportioning this number by known percentages reveals that each year there are about 3,800 freshman positions for the 150,000 high school graduates to fill, and about 2,400 college seniors to fill the approximately 64 positions for rookies in professional basketball. Thus, 2.6% (or less than 1 in 30) of high school seniors will progress to college basketball, one half that number will receive basketball scholarships, and only 2.7% (or 3 in 100) will make it for at least one year in professional basketball.

Similarly, according to the National Federation of State High School Associations (NCAA, 1990), each year there are approximately 265,000 seniors among the 927,000 high school students playing football, 47,000 NCAA intercollegiate football players in the country, approximately 16,450 new freshman positions available, 8,930 college seniors, and 215 positions available for rookies in the National Football League. These figures indicate that 6.2% (or 1 in 16) of high school football players progress to collegiate football and 3.1% (or 1 in 32) receive scholarships.

Essentially, less than 10% of the student athletes now participating in competitive sports will ever make it into the professional ranks, and of that less than 10%, 2% will receive injuries prohibiting their continued play, 3% will not be contracted to play for any extended period of time, and less than 1% will achieve superstardom. Ninety-five percent of all professional athletes have an average career span of 3 to 4 years and must eventually seek other employment, and 75% of that 95% depend on their new employment for survival. The reality is that students need to be better prepared to cope with life as it is, and not as they would wish it to be.

THE ROLE OF THE SCHOOL COUNSELOR

The following section is included for those readers who might not be familiar with the role of the school counselor. The American School Counselor Association's role statement on the school counselor published in 1990 references the appropriate role and function of the school counselor. The role described herein is based on that document (ASCA, 1990). The school counselor works with all students in the school, and the school counseling program is an integral part of the school's total educational program.

There are objectives, activities, special services, and expected outcomes, with an emphasis on helping students to learn more effectively and efficiently. School counselors are employed in elementary, middle/junior high, senior high, and postsecondary schools, and their work is differentiated by attention to age-specific developmental stages of growth and related interests, tasks, and challenges. They are human behavior and relationship specialists who organize their work schedules around fundamental interventions in a comprehensive developmental counseling program. The three most generally recognized and used forms of intervention are *counseling, consulting,* and *coordinating.*

Counseling is a complex helping process in which the counselor establishes a trusting and confidential working relationship. The focus is on problem solving, decision making, and discovering personal meaning related to learning and development. The counseling process involves individual counseling, small group counseling, and large group guidance.

Individual counseling is a personal and private interaction between a counselor and a student in which they work together on a problem of interest. A face-to-face, one-to-one meeting with a counselor provides a student maximum privacy to freely explore ideas, feelings, and behaviors and affords the school counselor the maximum opportunity to establish trust and build a helping relationship. School counselors are obligated by law and by ethical standards to explain the total parameters of the counseling relationship at the very beginning of the relationship. They must explain the meaning d ramifications of confidentiality, the extent to which confidentiality can be maintained, and their duty to report and refer a case when a person's welfare is in jeopardy. The school counselor is ethically bound to show respect for the privacy of information, always considering actions in terms of the rights, integrity, and welfare of students.

Group counseling involves a counselor working with two to eight students to remediate a common problem, concern, interest, or need. Small group counseling sessions may be relatively unstructured or based on structured learning activities. Group members have an opportunity to learn from each other, share ideas, give and receive feedback, increase their awareness, gain new knowledge, practice skills, and think about their goals and actions. Group discussions are generally problem centered, with attention given to particular concerns, or growth centered, with the focus on general topics related to personal and academic development.

Group guidance is generally conducted with a class and is preventative in nature. It is the counselor's best opportunity to provide guidance to the largest number of students in the shortest time. Group guidance sessions utilize cooperative learning methods to assist students in the acquisition of life skills. The counselor uses a guidance and counseling curriculum composed of organized objectives and activities that give attention to particular developmental issues or areas of concern (e.g., study skills, peer relationships, test-wiseness, self-concept, goal setting, and decision making). In this arena, counselors are implementors of group guidance sessions as well as resources and facilitators for classroom teachers, who should be an integral part of this guidance function.

Consultation is a process through which the counselor helps people be more effective in working with others. Consultation helps individuals think through problems and concerns, acquire more knowledge and skill, and become more objective and self-confident. This intervention can take place in individual or group conferences, or through staff development activities.

Coordination as a counselor intervention refers to the counselor's managing various services that benefit students and acting as a liaison between school and community agencies. It may include organizing special events that involve parents or resource people in guidance projects, collecting data and disseminating information, coordinating a student needs assessment, interpreting standardized tests, or organizing a child study team or a guidance-related teacher or parent education program.

IDENTIFYING STUDENT ATHLETES

Student athletes do not necessarily carry the "jockish" personas often attributed to them. While there are certain indices that distinguish the student athlete from other students, those indices are not always apparent. Aside from the more obvious physical manifestations exhibited by many student athletes, student athletes are often intense, are sometimes shy and reticent, can be eager to please, and are often loners and perceptually antisocial. By contrast, they can often be very liked by their peers. Their need to excel in sports might be transferred into their academic and personal lives, making them aggressive in all endeavors, or it can have the opposite effect, causing almost lethargic behavior in every domain except sports. Male student athletes are often sought after by the opposite sex, while female student athletes often intimidate males who are not sports enthusiasts.

Both male and female student athletes need fairly high self-confidence levels to combat the myriad of responses and reactions they receive from their contemporaries, their parents and siblings, the adult business world, and the public sports arena. However, adolescent student athletes frequently receive mixed messages and might become dependent upon outside sources to validate their identities, worth, and athletic prowess. This phenomenon can often cause skewed perceptions, unrealistic goals, and less-than-traditional value systems.

COUNSELOR RESPONSIBILITIES TO STUDENT ATHLETES

Student athletes require at least the same counseling services as other students do. As a segment of the at-risk population, however, athletes do have unique personal, vocational, and academic needs (as indicated by the literature and research as cited by Wittmer et al., 1981) which can and should be met through comprehensive strategic delivery of services by the school counselor.

The Student Profile

The school counselor should generate a student profile on each student counselee. This profile is generated in conjunction with an individual counseling session or in an academic advising session. It should include not only basic demographic information but also career interest, hobbies, talents, wish list, future aspirations, extracurricular activities, etc. This provides capsule information, indices of concern and interest on each student which can be easily referenced when opportunities or concerns present themselves.

Counselor Knowledge That Can Help Students

High and low self-esteem. The school counselor recognizes that the older the child is, the more his or her life will be affected by societal and peer pressures that can decrease the child's self-esteem. The student athlete is susceptible to extremes in many categories, so reaching a "happy medium" is often easier said than done. For validation of the self, the student athlete may depend solely on others, solely on himself or herself, or on some combination thereof. Self-esteem may be based primarily on sports performance in lieu of overall performance in life, and skewed, often corroborated, perspectives may prevent the acquisition of a healthy self-concept. The school counselor:

—Provides group guidance, group counseling, and individual counseling through the comprehensive developmental counseling program in such areas as:

values clarification	self-concept	coping strategies
peer relationships	decision making	stress management
self-awareness	interpersonal skills	goal setting
time management		

—Helps significant others to understand the pivotal role they play in the defining of self by the student athlete and to recognize the "space" parameters defined by student athletes, which can often help the significant others make positive contributions.

—Sensitizes others, such as faculty, students, staff, and parents, to the needs, circumstances, and feelings of the student athlete. Raises awareness levels through discussion and recognition and notes the critical imbalance that might occur and the need for the acquisition of a healthy self-concept by the student athlete.

—Conducts and/or initiates parent workshops and seminars. Provides opportunities for parents to network, dialogue, and gain a comfortable level of understanding relative to their children's developmental stages, goals, and decision-making processes. Provides parents the opportunity to role-play situations, vent angers and frustrations, and learn to cope with the realities of living with potential and want-to-be stars.

Stress and anxiety. The school counselor recognizes that stress is with us all the time, and that the secret to healthy stress is the ability to achieve balance between the stressors and the response to stressors (Herbert, 1983). Emotional effects of stress such as anxiety, depression, and hopelessness can result both from chronic stress and from specific traumatic events. For the student athlete, stress transcends the realm of the adolescent. Stressors are supplied by adults, students, and the environment and tend to be accepted and institutionalized as part of the milieu with which one must "deal" if one is to "make it." The school counselor:

—Conducts in-service workshops for faculty and staff on the consequences of stress on students and effective coping strategies to implement in the classroom, including relaxation training.

—Conducts group guidance sessions with classes and group counseling sessions with identified students to help students learn about (a) the causes and sources of stress, (b) the physiological and psychological reactions to stress, and (c) effective coping techniques.

—Works with students individually to help them understand stress, identify specific stressors, assess realistically, and learn effective coping strategies.

—Coordinates available community agencies and resources that can provide assistance, consultation, and appropriate referral placements for counselees.

Peer pressure. The school counselor recognizes peer pressure as a universal phenomenon that transcends age, color, race, ethnicity, and gender. Peer pressure thrives on the universal human need for acceptance and approval, and it is a leading cause of incidences of failure and irrational behavior experienced by students.

Student athletes are subjected to the pressures of peers in multiple arenas. School peers, team peers, and social peers all influence the student athlete and contribute to the list of stressors with which the student must cope. The natural maturation process, which can be difficult at best, is heightened by the effects and consequences of peer pressure and is often reported in less-than-pleasant terms by adolescents and young adults. And it is during adolescence that all students, especially student athletes, are most susceptible, because recognition and acceptance from peers often supercede principles held and rights understood by the sub-conscious.

Ultimately, however, one survives the pressures of peers through support and understanding from significant others such as parents, friends, peers, close associates, and authority figures. One must draw upon in-stilled values and beliefs to counteract the adverse effects often experienced via peer pressure. The school counselor:

—Provides opportunities for the student athlete to analyze behavior and the consequences of behavior in a safe environment; provides a medium for discussion, access to resources, and the potential to strategize plausible alternatives to the dilemma.
—Provides the opportunity for students to discuss concerns and experience commonality in individual and group counseling sessions.

Environmental factors. The school counselor recognizes the significance of environmental factors on student athletes. The media, coaches, teammates, peers, societal attitudes, academic systems, and athletic systems can all play heavily on the eventual success or devastation of student athletes, and it is the school counselor who could be most instrumental in remediating the process. Thus, the school counselor can make a significant contribution to the development of the student athlete by acting as coordinator for and consultant to the "athletic triangle" of athlete, coach, and parent (Goldberg, 1991). According to Goldberg, the promotion of a working alliance among these three has assumed special importance since, in many school districts, coaches are no longer members of the school's regular teaching staff and, consequently, may have little or no knowledge of the student athlete's in-school performance and little contact with the student in any role other than that of athlete. The school counselor:

—Provides academic advising regarding course requirements, college and career information, and test interpretation.
—Provides access to needed test instruments and preparation strategies for taking them.

CONCLUSION

School counselors have a definite responsibility to student athletes. Now more than ever, professional school counselors need to be assertive in alerting school systems, athletic departments, and parents that their specific skills are needed by student athletes. This is not to negate the need for athletic advisors, but rather to distinguish between the guidance function and the counseling function and to advocate for the two departments working together. The need for counseling professionals adept at analyzing human development, behavior, attitudes, and expectations to work harmoniously with athletics professionals is clear. The school counselor is in the unique position of serving as the preventative mental health specialist, whose goal of promoting positive mental health among student athletes is achieved by educating and collaborating with the people who influence their lives, as well as by assisting student athletes themselves to achieve psychologically healthy systems of values that transcend the athletic arena.

The following is a suggested counseling program. It contains the primary components for any comprehensive, developmental counseling program, and emphasizes the elements involved in working specifically with student athletes. However, all local school counseling programs should be tailored to the needs of the population based upon a current needs assessment.

A SCHOOL COUNSELOR'S PRACTICAL GUIDE: WORKING WITH STUDENT ATHLETES

A. Orientation and Articulation

1. Provide orientation for the student athlete as to the scope and parameters of the counseling program. Explain the modes of intervention used (individual and group counseling, group guidance, consultation, and coordination), the meaning and parameters of confidentiality, and the benefits to be gained by using the school counselor as a resource.

2. Sponsor orientation workshops for prospective student athletes, parents, coaches, and others as appropriate. Initiate a joint activity with the athletic department to stress the importance of guidance from the athletic department and counseling from the counseling department. Include such topics as: philosophy of school and department; benefits of program; potential sources of difficulty, burn-

out, and stress; requirements; nature and scope of roles for parents, coaches, and students. Also include topics such as lost class time, meeting schedules, make-up class rules, transportation, class attendance, and eligibility.

3. Explain that "articulation" refers to transition to the next progressive level (elementary to junior high, junior high to high school, and high school to college, military, or the world of work) and that the counselor's role is to help students understand the ramifications of the next level and to ensure a transition that is as smooth as possible. (Note: For student athletes, the transition may involve a new identity, a shift in behavioral expectations, a new set of skills, and new criteria for success.)

B. Developmental Component

1. Educational component

   a. Use group guidance sessions (with large groups and classes) to impart life skills which are preventative in nature. Sample topics: decision making, goal setting, peer relationships, study skills, test-wiseness, time management.

   b. Use group counseling sessions (with small groups of no more than 8 to 10) to remediate concerns presented by specific persons. Sample concerns: getting along with the opposite sex, family pressures, time management, setting goals, dealing with burnout and stress, communal living.

   c. Use individual counseling to discuss needs and remediate presenting concerns.

   d. Provide intensive academic advising for student athletes and their parents, addressing eligibility requirements for playing, course requirements and parameters for entering the next educational level, and coordination of schedules.

   e. Monitor student athlete profiles on a regular basis.

2. Vocational component

   a. Provide resources to aid students in finding current, viable information on career options.

   b. Provide information on appropriate assessment instruments of which students should avail themselves (ASVAB, SAT, PSAT, ACT, other interest inventories).

   c. Help students participate in career fairs and college fairs.

   d. Conduct or initiate the implementation of awareness seminars that focus on vocational information.

   e. Use statistical information from NCAA and other sources which supports the fact that only a few positions are actually available in professional sports.

      f. Coordinate a mentors/role-modeling program for student athletes using community resources.

C. Appraisal

1. Conduct test-wiseness sessions.
2. Conduct test interpretation workshops.
3. Work individually with students to analyze, interpret, and plan appropriately.

D. Adjustive Component

1. Work with identified students needing special assistance.
2. Initiate alternative modes of modifying behavior via individual contracts, alternative programs, etc.

E. Administrative Component

1. Maintain parent/student information centers with pertinent information relative to student athletes.
2. Administrate a comprehensive developmental counseling program.
3. Conduct/initiate workshops for parents and coaches inclusive of (a) developmental tasks confronting student athletes, and (b) critical roles parents and significant others play in student athletes' lives and the need for positive, responsible role modeling.
4. Work with athletic department to initiate controlled and monitored study hall periods and accessible tutoring and/or mentoring sessions during sports seasons.

F. Evaluation and Follow-Up

1. Conduct evaluations of various phases of the counseling program and make adjustments as appropriate via personal assessments, pre/post instruments, etc.
2. Design a method of follow-up on student athlete counselees.
3. Begin data base on students, collecting demographics, assessment instruments taken, scores, grades, anecdotal information, postgraduate interests, and postgraduate placements.

References

American School Counselor Association. (1990, December). ASCA defines role of the school counselor. *The ASCA Counselor*, pp. 10, 23.
Goldberg, A. D. (1991). Counseling the high school student athlete. *The School Counselor*, 38, 332–340.

Herbert, D. (1983). *Counseling youngsters for stress management.* Ann Arbor, MI: University of Michigan. (ERIC/CAPS Counseling and Personnel Services Clearinghouse No. ED 287-139)

Landers, D., Feltz, D., Obermeier, F., & Brouse, T. (1978). Socialization via interscholastic athletics: Its effects on educational attainment. *Research Quarterly, 49,* 475–483.

National Collegiate Athletic Association. (1990, February). *Probability of making a professional team in basketball or football.* Overland Park, KS: Author.

Wittmer, J., Bostic, D., Phillips, T. D., & Waters, W. (1981). The personal, academic, and career problems of college student athletes: Some possible answers. *The Personnel and Guidance Journal, 60,* 52–55.

CHAPTER 3

Issues in Counseling Athletes at the High School Level

SARA JOY BAILEY

Today's newspapers and sports magazines are filled with letters, articles, and editorials regarding the academic "plight" of the college athlete (e.g., Underwood, 1980). Colleges are attacked for "using" athletes, the NCAA is criticized for overregulating athletes (e.g., "Overreaction," 1991), and the athletes themselves are accused of being unmotivated, undisciplined, and disinterested in education (Harding, 1991).

The opinions as to who is responsible for creating the problems and who is responsible for solving them are equally varied. Advocates of a strong NCAA support tougher standards for scholarship athletes, while others advocate a lessening of restrictions to ensure fairness for all athletes. Critics of the colleges cite low graduation rates of athletes and demand more academic assistance and less emphasis on sports (e.g., Wakelee-Lynch, 1990). Other critics advocate treating athletes more like other students by, for example, abolishing athletic dormitories and special privileges.

But where does the athlete stand? Just how much responsibility belongs on his or her shoulders? Is the athlete a victim or a parasite? In response to the question of who is responsible for an athlete's physical skills development, most people would probably agree that, while the parents and coaches have some responsibility, the ultimate accountability must lie solely with the athlete. No one can "make" another individual develop athletic potential. If this is true in the physical realm, is it not also true in the academic realm? Naturally, others need to support, encourage, and teach, but the primary accountability must rest with the athlete. The NCAA cannot legislate, the institution cannot delegate, and the coach and parents cannot manipulate an athlete's academic success.

If the game truly is in the athlete's own hands, what can be done to promote academic excellence? The answer to this question lies in expediting the development of specialized skills: decision making, problem solving, time management, study and test taking, and self-discipline (Chartrand & Lent, 1987). Such skills are necessary for successful living, both within and without the world of sports. Colleges cannot use and abuse a student athlete who possesses self-knowledge, self-discipline, and self-confidence. But these qualities do not simply appear. They are the result of careful planning, nurturing, and maturing, the result of a cooperative effort among parents, coaches, teachers, counselors, and the athlete.

One final question remains: "When should such training begin?" The sooner it begins, the better. When an individual recognizes and begins to develop athletic ability, he or she should also begin to focus on those crucial personal and academic skills mentioned above. Too often parents and coaches wait to see if the athlete will be outstanding enough to be considered for athletic scholarships. By the time the answer is "yes," too much time has been wasted and the athlete must struggle both to enter and to succeed in college.

MYTHS AND REALITIES IDENTIFIED, DEFINED, AND EXAMINED

The topic "academics and athletes" sometimes evokes laughter and jokes, perhaps because the two are thought to be incongruous. The perceived incongruity can best be examined by considering the following six areas of concern:

1. Ability to perform academically
2. Maintenance of a balance between academics and athletics
3. Personal characteristics of athletes
4. Development of specialized academic skills
5. Expectations placed on athletes
6. Future plans of athletes

A look at the myths surrounding each of these areas may reveal some interesting new perspectives.

Ability to Perform Academically

One commonly held belief is that mental growth does not match physical growth in athletes. To examine this myth, consider any sport of your choosing. Select a successful, top-quality player. Ask yourself what mental abilities are required to play that position in that sport. The player probably must be able to learn complicated plays, to recognize and comprehend specific game situations, to analyze offensive and defensive strategies, to evaluate possible responses, and to make quick decisions. These mental abilities mirror those needed for success in the classroom. Motivation is a key in the transfer of such skills to the academic arena. While the motivation to be a great athlete may be intrinsic, the motivation to excel academically must often be fostered.

Maintenance of a Balance Between Athletics and Academics

A lack of time for study is often cited as a reason for poor grades. An article in the *Tennessee Secondary School Athletic Association News* addressing the effect of high school extracurricular activities (including athletics) points out that students who participate in activities make higher grades, have better attendance, and are better satisfied ("The Case," 1991). Also, coaches note that athletes tend to make better grades in season than they do out of season.

Sports do not necessarily consume too much of the student athlete's time. Being involved in sports does, however, challenge the student to manage his or her daily schedule wisely. Thus, time management skills are especially important to the successful student athlete.

Personal Characteristics of Athletes

When coaches and athletes are asked to identify the personal characteristics needed for success in sports, their lists include traits such as diligence, intelligence, positive attitude, dedication, endurance, determination, talent, self-motivation, and self-discipline. When teachers are asked to identify the personal characteristics vital to academic success, the list is exactly the same. Therefore, it must be conceded that the good athlete already possesses the personal characteristics needed to be a successful student. The issue is not whether the athlete is capable of succeeding in studies, but rather what needs to be done to expedite that success.

The Development of Specialized Academic Skills

If athletes possess the mental abilities and personal characteristics essential for academic success, it follows that what is lacking in those experiencing academic difficulty is simply a commitment to educational excellence and/ or a knowledge of study skills. In the physical realm, the athlete must work to mold his or her natural aptitude and physical prowess into the specialized skills needed for the chosen sport. Likewise, in the academic realm, the student athlete must develop some specialized study skills and habits that will strengthen academic performance.

Expectations Placed on Athletes

When asked "Why did you join a team for the first time?" many high school athletes answer, "Peer pressure." Richard Castallo noted six common sources of stress among athletes:

1. Poor preparation
2. Social distractions
3. Family crises
4. Financial stress
5. Confused career directions
6. Health concerns

(Castallo, 1986).

Joe Paterno cited two major problems of college athletes: coping with emphasis on winning combined with the temptations of early financial rewards, and coping with college work (National Association of College Admissions Counselors [NACAC], no date, p. 1). Are such expectations impossible to live up to? While the expectations may be potentially overwhelming, special efforts can be made to build a solid foundation of self-esteem, self-confidence, and self-worth. Armed with such a strong "self," the student athlete is better prepared to view the expectations as challenges rather than obstacles, and hence to handle them more constructively.

Future Plans of the Athlete

Why do athletes seem to have tunnel vision concerning the future and sports? Entire books have been devoted to this subject, and many "game plans" have been devised to assist athletes in making decisions about their futures. The book *Athlete's Game Plan for College and Career* states that "student athletes themselves often must share in the blame for neglecting the very important sides of their lives that reach beyond athletics" (Figler & Figler, 1984, p. ix). They must learn to anticipate life after competitive sport-playing (NACAC, no date, p. 1).

Regardless of which book is read or which strategy is chosen, decision making and problem solving are the basic skills needed. Why should an athlete wait until the question is a future after sports? These same skills are needed from the very beginning of athletic participation and should be taught early.

Kevin Ross, a college basketball player, is a highly publicized example of a student athlete who failed to balance athletics and academics. When he returned to junior high to learn basic skills after 4 years in college, he stated, "All those school years, I gave 150% in basketball and I got 50% of an education" (Figler & Figler, 1984, p. 80). Again, the question arises, "Who is to blame?" The answer is still the same: "Responsibility for the athlete's welfare is primarily up to the athlete" (Figler & Figler, 1984, p. 82). However, if this predicament of imbalance is to be avoided, every young athlete needs to be taught how to employ in the academic arena those attributes which are so commonly employed on the playing field.

A PRACTICAL SOLUTION

Like the weather, balancing athletics and academics is a subject "everybody talks about, but no one does a thing about." Almost everyone, from the fan in the stands to the college president, will discuss the problem and place the blame (e.g., Harding, 1991), but what is needed is a practical solution— a tried, proven, workable plan. The following model, "Athletes and Academics," has been used successfully with high school students for several years, and has been changed and expanded as the need has arisen. (Note: This project, implemented by the author at Whitehaven High School, Memphis, Tennessee, is continuing. The author is available for consultation.)

Personnel

An effective program must include everyone associated with the athlete, both at home and at school.

Counselors. The school counselor must be the leader of the team, the individual who plans and implements the activities. The counselor's enthusiasm and interest can make the difference between success and failure.

Coaches. The best planned program cannot succeed without the full support and cooperation of the coach. For example, often the coach must be willing to sacrifice practice time for academic skill-building activities.

Faculty. The teacher's contribution might include offering individualized assistance to one student, providing weekly progress reports, or actually teaching specific subject-related skills in special workshops. A cooperative faculty can make the program much more effective.

Parents. Unless an athlete's parents play an active role, that particular individual's chance for success is limited. At home, emotional support as well as actual monitoring of study are helpful in ensuring that the athlete practices the skills learned.

Athletes. The athlete is the key, for no one can force another individual to learn. A perfect program is of no benefit to an athlete who refuses to be mentally present and to participate in learning activities. If the desire to be a better student is lacking, all efforts are doomed.

Schedule

The "Athletes and Academics" calendar encompasses year-round activities.

Summer

An all-day workshop for both athletes and parents is conducted just prior to the opening of school. In this session, the emphasis is on preparing mentally for the coming school year.

Fall

1. *Parent meetings* are scheduled as needed. Emphasis is on keeping parents informed, especially regarding recruiting procedures, and teaching them how to become actively involved in their student's education.

2. *College entrance test preparation sessions* are conducted on a regular basis throughout both semesters. In addition, practice exams are offered on Saturdays. Coaches must be cooperative if the athlete is to get maximum benefit.

3. *Grade monitoring* includes a weekly progress report and an academic team meeting each grading period. A simple checklist, taken by the athlete to each teacher and given to the coach, encourages early intervention with potential problems. The team meeting is used to reinforce learning through additional activities and speakers.

4. *Coordination with college recruiters* involves maintaining a file of NCAA academic forms on senior athletes (with their permission) so that recruiters can know each athlete's academic standing. This allows the counselor to present each athlete in the most positive manner while building rapport with the college athletic departments. An additional benefit is that the athlete can be aware of his or her academic standing at all times.

5. *Special sessions* are arranged whenever particular situations or problems arise. Unique testing opportunities, team problems such as intersquad rivalry, trips to the state playoffs, and crises such as a team member's death are all situations demanding a quick response.

Spring

1. *Parent meetings* continue as needed. Seniors focus on evaluating college/scholarship opportunities. Sophomores and juniors concentrate on transcript evaluation and course selection for the following school year.

2. *Monitoring of grades* continues.

3. *Special sessions* continue as needed.

4. *Individual and group counseling* for spring registration is one of two major activities in the spring. The object is to ensure that each athlete is enrolled in those core courses required by the NCAA, but in courses appropriate for his or her level of achievement.

5. *Goal-setting sessions* are conducted for either teams or individuals. Emphasis may be on personal, athletic, or academic goals, whether short-term or long-term. Special focus is given to individual athletic goals for summer workouts. Specific physical goals are set, sealed, and stored until the summer workshop, when they are opened and progress is assessed. Also, at the beginning of each sports season, specific team goals are set.

Overview of the Program

What distinguishes this model from other programs is its specialized curriculum. While the various topics themselves are conventional, the presentation and content are designed to address the unique needs of athletes. There are six major components in the program:

1. Developing time-management skills
2. Building specialized academic skills
3. Setting goals
4. Learning decision-making and problem-solving processes
5. Developing interpersonal communication skills
6. Improving parent involvement

Developing Time-Management Skills. The claim "I don't have time" is perhaps the athlete's first line of defense in poor academic performance. There is some merit in the statement, because most do spend much of the time immediately after school at practice or in competition. Therefore, the emphasis in this area concerns four skills:

—identifying available time
—scheduling study time more effectively
—utilizing study time more efficiently
—recognizing and eliminating time wasters

Specific activities might include creating an assignment calendar, developing a study schedule, and locating and utilizing "short" periods of idle time.

Building specialized academic skills. Because athletes are by nature "physical" people who are seemingly more comfortable with physical movement than with intellectual quiet, the focus of this component is on study skills that are adapted for "physical" people. Such skills include:

—working more effectively and efficiently in short time frames
—learning how to utilize class time so as to reduce outside study time
—developing note-taking skills so that reading assignments become "study," thus eliminating the need for a second read to set up notes for test preparation
—learning how to build a positive rapport with teachers
—understanding the differences between reading and studying, between doing an assignment and studying, between homework and study, and between memorizing and learning

Specific topics include studying in and out of class, note taking, listening, using an assignment calendar, preparing for tests, and developing positive classroom behaviors.

Setting goals. Athletes often dream of playing "tomorrow," whether that be in high school, in college, or in the "pros," or of "becoming the star" (Lee,

1983). But, too often, they do not know how to build a firm foundation for
these dreams. This part of the specialized curriculum focuses on the *process*
of goal setting, which consists of the following elements:

—setting realistic goals
—assessing personal strengths and weaknesses
—identifying specific behaviors, tasks, and actions which lead to-
    ward the desired goal
—evaluating progress and reassessing actions

The skills are practiced on both physical and academic goals by teams and
by individuals.

Learning decision-making and problem-solving processes. From the very
beginning of an individual's participation in athletics, choices must be made—
"Will I play?" "Which sport?" "What team?" At first parents, coaches, and
peers exercise so much influence that the choices are not made consciously
by the athlete. As the athlete becomes more competitive and/or more proficient, the choices become more numerous and more difficult, culminating
in "Which college?" and "What career?" In this area the emphasis is on the
following processes:

—learning and using a decision-making/problem-solving model
—identifying outside influences and handling the resulting pressure
—setting priorities

Developing interpersonal communication skills. Teams function better when
communication among players is accurate and instantaneous. Likewise, students fare better when the level of communication with the teacher is open
and positive. As some athletes become more competitive, more successful,
and, hence, better known, the ability to communicate effectively becomes
even more critical. For these reasons this model includes a component to
assist students in the development of the following interpersonal communication skills:

—handling personal interviews
—listening effectively
—thinking "on your feet"
—learning to respond positively
—focusing on others
—building cooperation and team spirit

Improving parent involvement. Recognizing the critical role of the parent
in an athlete's physical and mental development, this model incorporates
some parental skill building. Efforts are made to encourage and teach parents

—to become more knowledgeable of a student athlete's academic
    standing and progress

—to stay informed concerning all rules and regulations affecting eligibility, scholarships, and recruiting
—to participate in the athlete's decision-making opportunities
—to help the athlete develop effective home study habits
—to monitor and assist with study time

Recommendations for Effective Implementation

As observed earlier, athletes tend to be more physically oriented, less inclined to sit and intellectualize. For this reason the format of all activities involves doing, not telling. Activities are active rather than passive, visual rather than oral, and practical rather than theoretical.

Many learning strategies are used to enhance motivation, learning, and retention. The more unusual the activity, the more effective it seems to be. Statistical information related to sports makes an attention-getting introduction. Brainstorming is another effective starting point.

Paper and pencil assignments, checklists, questionnaires, and continuums get the athlete involved in the activity and, at the same time, objectively assess personal skills, attitudes, and/or habits. Games, puzzles, or competitions of any sort not only aid in discovery learning but also appeal to the competitive nature of the athlete. Small group projects can teach cooperation and teamwork as well as a particular skill. Simulations, though more difficult to create, are especially effective activities. The use of visual aids is critical to better understanding and retention. Acrostics, gimmicks, mnemonics, and alphabetical guide words all make learning easier and more fun. The more directly the visual aid is related to the specific sport or to the school's mascot, the greater the interest level will be.

Sources for activities are found everywhere. Professional books and journals are more readily accessible. However, many general and sports-related magazines also contain ideas and information which can generate activities. Activities may also be adaptations of games or materials from unrelated sources. But the counselor's creativity provides the most inexhaustible supply.

CONCLUSION

The myths concerning athletes and academics can be dispelled if real effort is made for early intervention. Thus, the ultimate game plan of Athletes and Academics is to prepare student athletes for physical and academic competition at any educational level by helping them strengthen their academic skills and efforts. Perhaps the most rewarding outcome is that they learn to develop balance in their lives—a trait that will enable them to play the game of life with confidence and contentment long after they leave the playing field.

References

The case for high school activities. (1991, Spring). *Tennessee Secondary School Athletic Association News*, p. 15.

Castallo, R. (1986, September). Making the right choice: Guiding the high school student athlete. *Chronicle Guidance Publications, Inc.*, pp. 22–25.

Chartrand, J. M., & Lent, R. W. (1987). Sports counseling: Enhancing the development of the student-athlete. *Journal of Counseling and Development, 66*, 164–167.

Figler, S., & Figler, H. (1984). *Athlete's game plan for college and career*. Princeton: Peterson's Guides.

Harding, T. (1991, July 10). AAU basketball players get lesson on staying eligible. *The Commercial Appeal*, p. D-2.

Lee, C. C. (1983). An investigation of the athletic career expectations of high school student athletes. *The Personnel and Guidance Journal, 62*, 544–546.

National Association of College Admissions Counselors. (no date). *High school planning for college-bound athletes*.

Overreaction at the NCAA. (1991, July 5). *The Commercial Appeal*, p. A-6.

Underwood, J. (1980, May 19). The writing is on the wall. *Sports Illustrated*, pp. 36–45.

Wakelee-Lynch, J. (1990, May 24). Higher education's commitment to Black athletes questioned. *Guidepost*, pp. 1, 3–4.

CHAPTER 4

Role Models: An Athlete's Perspective

DICK BARNETT

Professional athletes are role models, particularly to the young and impressionable in American society. This chapter will describe an innovative program which uses athletes and other professionals as role models and change facilitators in the educational process.

The specific population under consideration here includes at-risk students and situational learners, who are influenced by a number of external elements in their daily lives, such as television, peer groups, street institutions, home, school, and church. These sociodynamic factors serve to affirm and reinforce patterns in the student's behavior.

At-risk students and situational learners display behavioral traits identified as leading indicators for dropping out or dropping behind in the educational process. Some of these indicators are frequent absenteeism, poor attention span, disciplinary problems, inadequate socialization skills, and cognitive underdevelopment.

Professional athletes are role models for at-risk students and situational learners for many reasons: (a) they excel at skills that children from low-income families can understand and imitate, unlike other professional or corporate success models, whose skills are mysterious to some underprivileged children; (b) they are highly visible because of the media attention given to their performances and to their "glamorous" personal lives and backgrounds; (c) their incomes are perceived as spectacular by at-risk children, for whom incomes of corporate and other professionals have little meaning or are unknown; (d) they frequently come from economic backgrounds similar to those of the children who admire and idolize them. Any concerned individual can urge young children to stay in school, to avoid drugs, and to prepare for the future, but children are more likely to "hear" these messages when they come from athletes the children seek to emulate. It is incumbent upon those who are concerned with the futures of situational learners and at-risk children to utilize the influence of professional athletes in the nurturance of those children.

LEARNING THROUGH MODELING

The professional athlete's exposure, popularity, and charisma have grown out of a historical backdrop of rugged individualism and a theory of manifest destiny. Ashe (1988) notes that the contemporary era of American sports began in 1946. World War II was over, many citizens had money in their pockets, and television was soon to become part of the culture. In the first 5 years of this period, baseball reasserted itself as the most popular spectator sport. Professional football merged two competing leagues and became stronger than before, and professional basketball went through similar adjustments. Since professional athletes' media exposure is now so widespread, their interaction with alienated at-risk children and situational learners in an educational environment can have a dramatic, positive impact.

Bandura (1977) contends that television, films, and other visual media provide abundant sources of social modeling. Through a phenomenon known as *symbolic modeling*, both children and adults acquire attitudes, emotional responses, and new styles of conduct by watching film and television. With the increasing use of symbolic modeling, parents and traditional role models may occupy less prominent roles in the social learning process.

Emerging from this learned behavioral response phenomenon is a methodology that educators, parents, and social behaviorists can utilize to improve children's cognitive, linguistic, and social development. This methodology utilizes a structured programmatic approach and a shared decision-making modality to maximize the attributes that professional athletes bring to the educational environment.

ATHLETIC ROLE MODEL EDUCATIONAL PROGRAM

Introduction

The development of the Athletic Role Model Educational Program was undertaken in response to the myriad problems and challenges in the educational system. The rationale of the program is rooted in the theoretical foundations espoused by Bandura (1977) and was reached through a committee group process.

The program is cognitive in nature and engages role models from a number of disciplines. Athletes are used as catalysts to galvanize the attention of situational learners, thereby offering the opportunity for cognitive development to take place. The role models are men and women from a variety of cultural and ethnic backgrounds, representing real-world professions such as computer analysis, law enforcement, business, entertainment, insurance, industry, medicine, academia, law, and, of course, professional sports.

The Athletic Role Model Educational Program has as its base the belief that every child can learn. It facilitates the development of cognitive skills, while providing historical and cultural reference points for children from every cultural group. Culture is one foundation upon which pride is built, and the struggles for dignity of those who have gone before them inspire children to learn. Survival takes on a collective consciousness. An imperative emerges to build families for the future, to establish community institutions, and to understand social, political, economic, educational, and cultural dynamics through a pluralistic world view.

Orientation

Because the Athletic Role Model Educational Program for at-risk students and situational learners utilizes professional athletes, it is paramount that educators, parents, students, and private sector participants step outside of the stereotypes that have been imposed on professional athletes. In order for the program to be effective, its participants must dispense with the "all brawn, no brains" notion, and must take into consideration the competitive leadership qualities of athletes and help direct their enormous popularity, exposure, and charisma toward facilitating learning.

The intergroup approach is indispensable in the Athletic Role Model Educational Program. The program must seek out and bring into the planning, developmental, and designing phases all those who directly or indirectly affect the lives of at-risk children and situational learners. Administrators, teachers, parents, private sector participants, and professional athletes and other positive role models must collaborate to discuss, formulate, crystallize, and finally agree on a programmatic strategy to integrate a role model program into the classroom. These intergroup processes should be coordinated by committees. Committees can be segmented by groups (e.g., teachers with teachers) or integrated (e.g., teachers with administrators). Out of these committee deliberations should emerge a variety of recommendations for review, consideration, possible pilot observation, and finally confirmation, by consensus of all the committee groups.

The Role of Professional Athletes in the Program

Professional athletes are vital in the change process for at-risk students and situational learners. The athletes are revered, imitated, and admired among members of every strata of society. Their exposure, mass media coverage, and celebrity status enhance their acceptance among youngsters, and they usually enjoy an excited, alert, and motivated audience. As educators and communities encourage participation by these experts, they will be in a tremendous position to provide not only the catalyst for the program, but leadership as well.

Professional athletes are well equipped to elicit needed support and resources for the program. For instance, they might contact businesses in the community, or provide a forum to focus media attention on a particular problem. They can also help alert and unite the legislature, chancellors, and superintendents in their quest to expand the educational experience.

Instructional Strategies and Activities

The Athletic Role Model Educational Program articulates differing approaches in its design to accommodate the learning styles and strategies necessary to build on those internal and external factors that children bring into the classroom. A diverse approach considers all of the perceptive senses in this process. Observation, hearing, touching, speaking, movement, and manipulation are implemented. The educational component of the program utilizes the following innovations and strategies: appropriate technology, large-screen monitors, model-to-student exchange lines, field trips, classroom presentations, electronic newsletters, computerized lesson plans, demonstration projects, career development workshops, videotape and audiotape, expositions, question and answer sessions, rap sessions, debates, lectures, and research projects. The role model strategies that are used in the presentations and discussions are cognitive-based strategies that include modeled behavior that can be transformed into writing, reading, math, science, and history lessons.

Materials

A number of materials have been identified as appropriate for students' development in the role model program. The following are just a few examples:

> posters (historical references)
> bulletin boards
> video text
> role model library
> computers
> high-definition television
> films

These materials will not only give positive signals about at-risk students and situational learners, but will also provide the cognitive rigor necessary to expand their abilities to communicate, think, and problem-solve, and stimulate the development of a sense of self. Some materials are already on the market, but the Role Model Educational Program will also develop new instructional strategies and materials through the intergroup process and as an outgrowth of role model presentations.

Books and other media, such as pamphlets and newspaper and magazine articles, will be used as well. The literature will cover a wide range of subjects, including the arts, civil rights, sports, history, business, media, and government.

Role Models

The Athletic Role Model Educational Program is an intervention modality that seeks to influence the behavior of situational learners and at-risk students through the methodologies of observational learning, identity formation, and special learning theories. Bandura (1977) postulates that children learn and do what they see others do. His theory expands tremendously in application by positive role models. Their behavior, through mass media instruments, can reach millions of people at any given time. Bandura's data maintain that such exposure brings about symbolic interaction in situational learners.

Technology

The Athletic Role Model Educational Program should be steeped in 21st-century technical capability. High-resolution monitors will be expanded to include video presentations, live on-line exchanges between students and role models, live and tape-delayed lesson plans, and curriculum development. Computers can be used to develop community bulletin boards, increased telecommunications networking, business/student technology centers, internship opportunities, apprenticeships, and orientations. The use of technology and instant communication is confined only by the limitations of the current state of the technology and by the decisions of how and when to make that technology available to students.

Staff Development

Staff development and training must have a significant priority if success is to be achieved. A training program for teachers, athletes, and private sector role models will provide the time and environment for them to develop ownership in the proposed program and acquire needed skills. Support and familiarity will assist teachers, athletes, and private sector models to nurture interpersonal relationships with at-risk students and situational learners.

The following orientation strategies will provide hands-on experience with the role model concept:

1. Orientation to develop the kinds of topics and approaches that will stimulate student interest and full participation by models.
2. Workshops to provide demonstrations of how role models would fulfill leadership and motivational functions in classroom situations.

3. Seminars to exchange vital ideas and methodologies that may be
   of merit (rap sessions, demonstrations, story telling, biographical
   profiles).
4. Live demonstrations of the kind of technology proposed for use
   in the role model program.

Workshops

Through presentations and visual technology, models will help illuminate
the various aspects of differing cultures and experience, leading the students
to a fuller understanding of the ways in which divergent groups have contributed to the development of the American perspective. Projects will include short stories, biographical profiles, essays, poetry, and question and
answer sessions.

The role models will confer regularly with teachers regarding the direction and dimensions of the role-model-to-student interactions. There will
be comprehensive, hands-on orientation sessions to develop and design strategies that will inspire students to imitate modeled behavior. The orientation
sessions need to include demonstration workshops which help focus the
participation of role models into a cognitive experience and highlight the
ability of role models to influence student behavior.

Change Strategy

Hall and Hord (1987) have developed a strategy to assist the change process.
Their model, the Concerned-Based Adoption Model, utilizes *change strategy*, a methodology based on the idea that change is a process, not an event.
The model determines the capacity of teachers and administrators to accept
change in intervention and alternative programs. It serves as an awareness
instrument so that change facilitators can gauge the amount of resistance to
change and develop appropriate strategies to adapt to that resistance. The
Concerned-Based Adoption Model is utilized (a) to make teachers aware of
the program, its features, its participants, and its objectives; (b) to calculate
levels of resistance to a new program; (c) to monitor personal and collective
professional concerns; and (d) to solicit questions, proposals, and recommendations concerning the design of the role model innovation.

For schools and students to improve, teachers must change. For teachers to change, they must be called upon to develop, adopt, or adapt to
appropriate and promising innovations.

Evaluation

In the Role Model Educational Program, monitoring and evaluation processes occur concurrently. Evaluation takes place in a continually changing
environment which reflects social, political, and economic processes. Some

types of changing circumstances which can have an effect on program evaluation are:

1. The relative influence, resources, and priorities of educators.
2. Changes in the interests and influence of the various change facilitators.
3. Marked modifications in the priorities and responsibilities of the organizations and school agencies implementing programs.
4. Unanticipated problems with delivering the intervention or with the intervention itself.
5. Partial funding from an evaluation, resulting in the reasonably secure knowledge that the intervention will not produce the intended outcomes.
6. Unanticipated problems in implementing the evaluation design.

CONCLUSION

The Athletic Role Model Educational Program is based on the premise that all children can learn, though not always in the same way or at the same rate. The program is rooted in a pluralistic philosophy, taking into consideration culture, history, and the social, political, economic, and educational dynamics that influence students' past and present behavior in school. This intervention strategy for at-risk students and situational learners is innovative in its approach and seeks to motivate and inspire students to remain in the educational process.

The program utilizes and expands available materials and technology, and creates modalities for using instructional activities. Positive role models provide the program with ingredients that may appeal to the sensitivity and learning styles of different students. The involvement of professional athletes, whose charisma and leadership infuse the learning environment with excitement, is a vital aspect of the program.

The Athletic Role Model Educational Program is one initiative developed by the Athletic Role Model Educational Institute. One such program currently operates in New York, and another is soon to be implemented in Gary, Indiana. The Institute is located at 305 Madison Avenue, Suite 1166, New York City, 10165, (212) 753-7235. The founder and president of the Institute is Dr. Dick Barnett.

References

Ashe, A. (1988). *A hard road to glory: A history of the African-American athlete– 1919–1945*. New York: Warner Books.

Bandura, A. (1977). *Social learning theory*. Englewood Cliffs, NJ: Prentice-Hall.

Hall, G. E., & Hord, S. M. (1987). *Change in schools*. New York: State University of New York Press.

CHAPTER 5

Coaches and Student Athletes

GARY M. MILLER

In examining the responsibilities placed on coaches of student athletes, Dr. Rainer Martens, an internationally known coaching educator, noted three major areas for consideration: (a) having a winning team; (b) helping players have fun; and (c) assisting in the development of athletes in the physical, psychological, and social aspects of their lives (Martens, 1990). To successfully take on all of their responsibilities to student athletes, coaches must be proficient in their sports as well as in the interpersonal skills necessary to function with the athletes and with their parents. Veller (1968) has noted that the coach "must remember at all times that he has in his hands the parents' greatest possession, their offspring" (p. 57). This chapter will address how the coach can play a role in promoting the development of the student athlete both as an individual and as a participant in a sport.

CRITICISM OF COACHES IN THE 20TH CENTURY

Concerns about the status of athletics in our society and the roles played by coaches have been discussed throughout the 20th century. In the early history of the century, athletics were extensively scrutinized and coaches came under attack. Griffith (1922) stated as follows:

> In the first place, we have not lived down the reputation that certain
> coaches of an earlier day gave to the game. The coaching fraternity of
> the present is for the most part made up of men of character whose
> ideals will compare favorably with the ideals of men in other profes-
> sions and in business. It will take some time, however, to correct the
> impression which now prevails. (p. 15)

43

Griffith was concerned about coaches at the high school and collegiate levels and their impact on the athletes of their time. Also in 1922, Bachman commented on the character of college football coaches.

> Happily the "win-at-all-cost coach," who teaches or permits his team to make use of unfair tactics during contests, or who encourages and winks at certain violations of the eligibility rules governing intercollegiate contests in which his team is engaged, that type of coach is rapidly disappearing. (1922, p. 24)

The hope soon developed that members of the coaching profession would take control of monitoring their own behavior and that of their peers. Griffith urged that "athletic coaches must of their accord, correct any evil which may exist in their institutions" (1922, p. 15). Apparently such self-monitoring has not evolved in intercollegiate sports. Athletics programs are in a state of change. The report of the Knight Foundation Commission on Intercollegiate Athletics (1991) has emphasized the need for college and university presidents to take the responsibility and authority for administering the athletics programs on their campuses. The presidents of higher education institutions are now challenged to correct the "evils" noted by Griffith.

COACHING PHILOSOPHIES AND LEADERSHIP STYLES

As Lapchick and Slaughter (1989) have noted, more than 20 million youngsters participate in youth sports programs, and about 3.3 million boys and 1.3 million girls participate in high school sports. Each of these young people will relate to a person called "Coach." The personal characteristics, philosophies, and leadership style of the coach can have a strong impact on the young athlete's development.

Various authors have presented their views of how coaches can positively influence the student athlete's personal development. For instance, Lombardo (1987) points out that coaches can facilitate the development of self-esteem in their players by focusing on the sports experience as "a vehicle to satisfy the needs of the athletes, as well as an activity with the potential to strengthen the athletes' feelings of self worth" (p. 37). To foster growth in self-esteem, the coach needs to believe in the athlete's ability to act responsibly and to develop appropriate goals. Ogilivie (1973), noting that the "incapacity for trust usually stems from early experiences which have conditioned the athlete to expect frequent betrayal" (p. 102), points out that coaches must be aware of the athlete's need to develop a sense of trust. Pietrofesa and Rosen (1968) criticize the overemphasis that is often placed on winning, and advocate placing a higher premium on the development of sportsmanship.

In general, effective team leaders are people who can set goals, create change, and induce others to follow them (Larson & LaFasto, 1989). These leadership traits manifest themselves in different ways depending on the individual coach's preferred style. According to Calhoun (1987), a coach's level of authoritarianism is determined by the coach's personality, by the degree of pressure to win, and by the number of authoritarian and democratic influences impinging upon the coach. Martens (1990) suggests that three relatively distinct coaching styles predominate: *command*, *submissive*, and *cooperative*. The command coach dictates to players, the submissive coach acquiesces, and the cooperative coach shares decision making with team members. Obviously, the cooperative style can do much to instill a sense of responsibility in individual team members.

TECHNIQUES FOR EFFECTIVE COACHING

Numerous strategies have emerged to help coaches examine how they can communicate with and relate to their athletes. Rosenfeld and Wilder (1990) have promoted active listening for improving communication among coaches, athletes, and parents. Lyon (1973, p. 86), addressing coach-to-athlete communication, suggests three major questions the coach must consider:

1. How do I know what I am communicating to the athlete?
2. How do I communicate what I know?
3. How do I know that I am getting across to the athlete?

Smith (1986) believes feedback can be useful to the student athlete in terms of performance enhancement and goal setting. According to Smith, feedback should focus on a specific behavior, the proficiency level to be attained, and the present performance level. Through such feedback the athlete and the team can work together to meet team and individual goals. As Larson and LaFasto (1989) have written, "if the goal is clear, worthwhile, and challenging, team members will probably do a better job of energizing and commanding themselves and fellow team members than will sources above or outside the team" (p. 139).

Rosenfeld and Wilder (1989) recommend a sandwich technique for giving feedback to athletes. They suggest that coaches first give positive feedback, then present new information to the athletes for improvement, and finish by offering encouragement directly related to the outcome sought. This technique can help in examining the goals the athlete has set as well as examining the actual physical attempt of a skill by the athlete.

When Tharp and Gallimore (1976) studied the teaching style of John Wooden, the famous basketball coach of the University of California at Los Angeles, they discovered that 50.3% of his verbal interaction with players involved instruction-oriented statements. They also noted that when coach Wooden demonstrated skills to his players, he rarely spent more than 5 seconds in the demonstration. His technique was to first show the correct method, then the incorrect method, then the correct method again. Galloway (1971) has noted that when communicating with an athlete one must remember that "to concern ourselves with nonverbal language is to take an attitude toward the importance of what people do rather than what they say" (p. 71). Perhaps this is why coach Wooden used demonstrations that featured both correct and incorrect ways of executing a skill.

COACHES AND PARENTS

In a coach's relationship with the parents of athletes, the need for two-way communication is critical (Smoll, 1986). Often the main area of conflict revolves around the different perceptions coaches and parents have about the athlete's abilities. Coaches are encouraged to meet with parents, without the athlete present, and discuss the issues in dispute. The coach should have some class performance indications that can be used for feedback to the parents and should listen nondefensively to the concerns voiced by the parents (Smoll, 1986).

Rosen (1978) has posed some thought-provoking questions for parents who wish to have their children participate in organized sports.

1. Can you give your child up and put him or her in the hands of the team's coach?
2. Can you admit your inabilities in the particular sport your child has selected?
3. Can you accept the success of your athlete?
4. Can you accept the disappointment of your athlete?
5. Can you, if you are coach as well as parent, demonstrate self-control?
6. Can you give your athlete some time?
7. Can you let your child make his or her own decision?

Parents, if they hope to play a positive role, must seriously consider these questions as they begin and progress through the athletic journeys of their child. Smoll (1986) believes parents and coaches need to consider what the parent's role can be regarding the athletic child. He recommends that children be advised about the sport they wish to enter and the level of competition to be faced. Parents need to be alerted to the tendency to overidentify with the child and the possible negative impact this may have. Parental behavior should also be discussed, with the understanding that the coach has the responsibility for the team and the parents are responsible for their own behavior at the athletic event (Smoll, 1986).

Martens (1990) has developed a complete parent orientation program, in which the coach attempts to help the parents understand the program and the objectives for the season. During the orientation, parents get acquainted with personnel who will be working with the student athletes, and gain a clearer understanding of the risks involved in the sport. Meetings between parents and coaches should clarify the responsibilities of the athlete and parents, as well as provide an opportunity for parents to discuss some of their concerns. In addition, communication channels can be developed during the meetings. The coach should also clarify the rules and any changes in rules from the previous year, including the procedures that will be incorporated in practices and during competition.

EXPECTATIONS FOR COACHES

Student athletes who begin participation at an early age and progress through the sports system develop expectations regarding coaches. LaGrand (1973) conducted a comprehensive study of what athletes seek in a coach. A sample of 304 athletes from 13 colleges rated coaches on 14 specific characteristics. The highest-rated item was the coach's knowledge of the sport. Enthusiasm was the next highest rated item, with the willingness to help athletes and demanding hard work being rated third and fourth in importance.

Surveying gymnasts, Massimo (1980) found that the less skilled gymnasts sought coaches who had technical knowledge, whereas the more skilled gymnasts sought coaches who would provide emotional support. The high-level performers wanted a coach who was willing to get to know them. Both the accomplished gymnasts and the not-so-accomplished gymnasts viewed the effective organization of training and a real love of the sport as important elements.

The author recently was placed on an advising committee for selecting a basketball coach at a university where the coach of the previous four seasons had been dismissed. When the team's players were asked what traits they wanted in a new coach, the following ones emerged: honesty, compatibility, willingness to listen, and a genuine concern for the players. A group of high school coaches, questioned by the author, listed the following as crucial aspects of their role in working with student athletes:

1. Stress academics.
2. Present high school and college requirements.
3. Set a positive example.
4. Develop communication skills with student athletes and their parents.
5. Inform student athletes regarding life after athletics.

From the perspective of a group of school counselors, coaches of student athletes should strive to:

1. Promote good sportsmanship.
2. Develop values focusing on a positive work ethic and a team effort.
3. Support counselors in helping student athletes achieve academic success.
4. Be role models.
5. Care for the individual.
6. Communicate with parents about the student athletes and their need to be successful in many aspects of their lives.

It appears that in the eyes of athletes, coaches, and counselors there is more to the athletic equation than winning, although winning is important. Human development involves the personal aspects of the student athlete as well as the physical aspects of the person. Coaches who work with student athletes need to help them examine the meaning of athletics in their lives. In doing so, a relationship can be established in which the coach can help the student plan for athletic success as well as for success as a student, a person, and a member of society.

NEW PROGRAMS FOR ASSISTING STUDENT ATHLETES

In many cases, coaches and school counselors have worked together to develop programs to enhance their work with student athletes. For example, at South Aiken High School in South Carolina, the women's basketball and volleyball coach and a school counselor have developed a proposal for a one-credit course focusing on the academic and career development of student athletes. This proposal was recently approved by their local school district and is currently under final development.

In upstate New York at Jamesville-Dewitt High School, two high school counselors, one of whom also coaches basketball at a nearby inner-city high school, have developed a program for high school student athletes and their parents to prepare these young people for the realities of playing sports beyond high school. Through the seminar they conduct, information is given regarding current NCAA recruitment regulations and academic requirements.

At Irmo High School, near Columbia, South Carolina, the school's tennis coach and a school counselor have worked together to assess the personality traits of masculine instrumentality and female expressiveness in tennis team members. Through their research, they are working toward helping the players learn more about their individual traits and develop an understanding of how these traits can benefit them in tennis as well as in their daily interactions with others.

In an effort to acquaint incoming high school athletes in Bennettsville, South Carolina, with the realities that lie ahead of them, the head football coach and athletic director of Marlboro County High School and two counselors have developed seminars in which they discuss academic expectations, the 4-year academic plan, core courses required for college entrance, NCAA requirements, and career development. Student athletes and their parents are encouraged to set realistic expectations for the future. As part of the program, former college athletes present their views of what the student athlete experience was like for them. They alert students to the pitfalls one can encounter when athletics are overemphasized and academics and career development are set aside. The frank discussion by the former collegians provides a healthy reality-check for the high school students.

CONCLUSION

It is necessary for coaches to involve themselves in many aspects of the lives of their student athletes. Their young players are multidimensional individuals, and as coach Jack Bicknell (1989) has said,

> the most important aspect of this job is that we are working with young people, . . . who need understanding, discipline and better-experienced people to care about their future. (p. 150)

References

Bachman, C. W. (1922). Is football an asset to the college? *Athletic Journal*, 2(6), 22–28.

Bicknell, J. (1989). The coaching responsibility. In R. E. Lapchick & J. B. Slaughter (Eds.), *The rules of the game: Ethics in college sports* (pp. 137–150). New York: Macmillan.

Calhoun, D. W. (1987). *Sport, culture and personality* (2nd ed.). Champaign, IL: Human Kinetics.

Galloway, C. M. (1971, January). Teaching is more than words. *Quest*, pp. 67–71.

Griffith, J. (1922). Editorial comments. *Athletic Journal*, 3(2), 14–15.

Knight Foundation Commission on Intercollegiate Athletics. (1991). *Keeping the faith with the student-athlete: A new model for intercollegiate athletics*. Charlotte, NC: Author.

LaGrand, L. (1973). What athletes look for in their coaches. *Scholastic Coach*, 43(3), 92, 94.

Lapchick, R. E., & Slaughter, J. B. (Eds.). (1989). *The rules of the game: Ethics in college sports*. New York: Macmillan.

Larson, C. E., & LaFasto, F. M. J. (1989). *Teamwork*. Newbury Park, CA: Sage.

Lombardo, B. J. (1987). *The humanistic coach*. Springfield, IL: Charles C Thomas.

Lyon, L. P. (1973). Psychology of sport: Coach-athlete communication. *Scholastic Coach*, 43(3), 86–89.

Martens, R. (1990). *Successful coaching* (2nd ed.). Champaign, IL: Human Kinetics.

Massimo, J. (1980). The gymnast's perception of the coach: Performance competence and coaching style. In R. M. Guinn (Ed.), *Psychology in sports methods and applications* (pp. 229–337). Minneapolis: Burgess.

Ogilivie, B. C. (1973). Trust, the most basic insight. *Scholastic Coach*, 43(2), 102–103.

Pietrofesa, J. J., & Rosen, A. (1968, November). Interscholastic sports, misdirected? misguided? or misnomer? *The Clearing House*, 43(3), 156, 165, 169.

Rosen, A. (1978). Advice for fathers. In R. Martens (Ed.), *Joy and sadness in children's sports* (pp. 320–326). Champaign, IL: Human Kinetics.

Rosenfeld, L., & Wilder L. (1990). Active listening. *Sport Psychology Training Bulletin*, 1(5), 1–8.

Smith, R. E. (1986). Principles of positive reinforcement and performance feedback. In J. M. Williams (Ed.), *Applied sport psychology* (pp. 35–46). Palo Alto, CA: Mayfield.

Smoll, F. L. (1986). Coach-parent relationships: Enhancing the quality of the athlete's sport experience. In J. M. William (Ed.), *Applied sport psychology* (pp. 47–58). Palo Alto, CA: Mayfield.

Tharp, R. G., & Gallimore, R. (1976, January). What a coach can teach a teacher. *Psychology Today*, pp. 75–78.

Veller, D. (1968). Vital relationships for the coach. *Athletic Journal*, 49(3), 54–57, 69–71.

CHAPTER 6

A Guide for College-Bound Athletes

GARY A. SAILES

Each year, thousands of high school athletes will be recruited by college coaches to participate in intercollegiate athletics. Approximately two thirds of those prospective recruits will be offered full scholarships to meet the expenses of a college education, in exchange for their participation in varsity sports. The decision to attend college under such conditions is a major one requiring careful and serious thought. The decision will have an impact on the student athlete for the next 4 to 5 years and quite possibly for the remainder of his or her life. This chapter will provide basic information to be used in helping the student athlete select a suitable college or university, one that will further the student's educational and athletic goals.

ELIGIBILITY

In order to be eligible to participate in intercollegiate sports or to receive an athletic scholarship at an NCAA school, the student athlete must graduate from high school, and must have maintained a minimum grade point average of 2.0 in a core curriculum that includes at least 3 years of English, 2 years of mathematics, 2 years in the social sciences, and 2 years in the natural or physical sciences. In addition, he or she must achieve a minimum score of 700 on the Scholastic Aptitude Test (SAT) or a minimum score of 17 on the American College Test (ACT).

The SAT or ACT must be taken on a national testing date. Scores from residual or regional tests are not allowable. Student athletes should check with their school guidance counselor to find out the national testing dates for the ACT and SAT. It is advisable that they take the test early in the junior year of high school, to allow for retesting in the event of an initial failure to meet the minimum score required for college eligibility. A student athlete failing to meet any of the prescribed requirements would be ineligible to receive an athletic scholarship, would not be allowed to practice or compete with the college team, and would forfeit 1 year of eligibility. The student athlete could still be admitted to the school, and would retain 3 years of eligibility beginning in the sophomore year, provided he or she maintained at least a C average in 24 credit hours of course work during the freshman year.

Sailes (1990) showed only 5% of all recruited student athletes failed to meet the minimum eligibility requirements established by the NCAA. Most athletes who failed to meet the NCAA's minimum requirements did poorly on the SAT and ACT tests. Generally, African Americans and individuals from socioeconomically disadvantaged families do poorly on such standardized testing instruments (Crouse & Trusheim, 1988). It is highly recommended that college-bound student athletes begin preparation for the tests early in their sophomore year of high school.

PROFESSIONAL STANDING

The student athlete should be careful not to endanger college eligibility by becoming a professional. The NCAA does not allow professionals to compete in college athletics. The guidelines regarding participation in professional sports are explicit:

1. The student athlete is not allowed to receive monetary compensation or accept the promise of compensation for participating in an athletic contest.
2. The student athlete may not sign a contract or verbally commit with an agent or a professional sports organization.
3. The student athlete may not request that his or her name be placed on a draft list or otherwise agree to negotiate with a professional sports organization.
4. The student athlete may not accept payment in any form for athletic performances (for example, television commercials or demonstrations).
5. A student athlete may not play on a professional team.
6. A student athlete participating on an amateur sports team may not receive, directly or indirectly, any salary, incentive payment, award, gratuity, educational expenses, or expense allowances (other than those for actual and necessary travel and room and board).

Before enrolling in college, the student athlete is allowed the following by the NCAA:

1. To try out (practice but not participate against outside competition) with a professional sports team.
2. To receive actual and necessary expenses from any professional sports organization for one visit per professional organization not in excess of 48 hours.
3. To receive a fee for teaching lessons in a particular sport. (National Collegiate Athletic Association, 1991).

RECRUITMENT

The recruitment of high school student athletes by college coaches is regulated. The rules governing visits to prospective recruits by coaches are a little confusing but very explicit. There are different time periods when no contact is permitted, when coaches are allowed to watch a player but cannot talk to him or her, when indirect contact (mail or telephone calls) is permitted, and when direct contact (i.e., a personal visit by the coach) is permitted. The dates vary for each sport. No coach is allowed direct contact with student athletes until after they have completed their junior year of high school.

Student athletes and their parents should consult with high school coaches, who are usually aware of the rules regarding recruitment by college coaches. Any college coach making illegal contact with a high school athlete should be reported to the high school coach and to the national association of which the coach is a member. Coaches who make illegal contact or who violate any recruitment rules should be avoided, and the schools they represent should be removed from consideration by the student athlete. The athlete endangers eligibility by having contact with such coaches, and their unethical conduct is probably reflective of the programs they represent.

Generally, a coach will learn about a particular athlete through the media, from high school coaches, or through professional scouting reports. The scouting reports rate each athlete both athletically and academically. If a coach is interested in a student athlete, the head coach or assistant coach will visit the athlete's school or a sports camp to watch the athlete compete. Smaller colleges with little money for travel may request a videotape of the student competing in an athletic contest.

Once the recruiting process begins, an outstanding student athlete can be inundated with solicitations from different schools. As was mentioned, those solicitations can range from letters, phone calls, and scouting contacts to personal visits from head or assistant coaches. It is the primary job of any recruiter to sell the college or university to the prospect. In some cases, illegal inducements (such as cash, cars, and gifts), flattery and praise, and misrepresentations about the school or the athletic program can confuse both the student athlete and the parents, influencing them to make a poor selection. It is recommended that all recruitment efforts be screened through a central person (coach, guidance counselor, parent, experienced adult) to ensure that reputable and suitable schools are selected during the narrowing-down phase of the recruiting process.

SCHOLARSHIPS

When a coach is ready to commit to a prospect, the coach will offer an athletic scholarship. A typical college athletic scholarship covers expenses for tuition, room, board, fees, and books. Most athletic scholarships are guaranteed for 1 year and are renewable each year, at the discretion of the coach and/or athletic department, for a maximum of 5 years within a 6-year period. However, the conditions of athletic scholarships are negotiable, particularly for heavily recruited "blue chip" athletes. It is strongly recommended that the student athlete's coach, parents, and other experienced adult relatives and/or friends be involved in the negotiation of the terms of the scholarship. Lederman (1991) reported that after 5 years of college, approximately 56% of all student athletes, compared to 48% of all students, will graduate. It is in the best interest of the student athlete, then, to negotiate for a full scholarship that will cover all academic expenses until the student graduates, even if that takes longer than the 4 years of eligibility allowed by the NCAA.

NATIONAL LETTER OF INTENT

If a student is willing to accept an athletic scholarship to attend a specific college or university, the recruiting coach will usually require the student to sign a contract called a "National Letter of Intent." This letter of intent is a binding legal contract between the school and the student athlete. It is a serious commitment requiring careful consideration. Once the letter of intent is signed, the student athlete is committed to attend that school and may only be released from the contract by an official in the school's athletic department. If a student signs a letter of intent to attend a specific school and discovers the school or its athletic program does not suit his or her needs, the student may transfer to another school but will lose eligibility. It is imperative that the student athlete be absolutely certain about the choice of a school before signing a letter of intent. (See chapter 15 for more information on the letter of intent.)

VISITATIONS

Before accepting an athletic scholarship or signing a letter of intent, the student should visit the schools of interest. The NCAA allows the student athlete to make one visit each to five different schools, at the expense of the school. The visit may not exceed 48 hours. The student athlete and parents may receive only food and lodging, and may be entertained by the athletic staff.

The campus visit is probably the most crucial aspect of the recruiting process. The student athlete and the parents should utilize this time to learn as much as possible about the school and the athletic program. They should collect and read various literature about the school, talk to several students, athletes, coaches, faculty members, and administrators, and inspect the classroom, library, dormitory, and athletic facilities.

SELECTING A COLLEGE

Selecting a college is a time-consuming and difficult process. Careful thought and planning are required to narrow down the choices and select the school that best meets the needs of the student athlete. Throughout the process, priorities should be established and firmly maintained. Parents and students should consider various factors, such as geographic location, urban or rural setting, size of student body, academic and athletic reputations, graduation rates of all student athletes, and graduation rates of student athletes in the student's particular sport. The reputation of the department that houses the student's chosen major is also an important consideration. Other concerns include the school's career placement office's record for locating employment for graduating students, scholarship guarantee in the event of injury whether it is sports-related or not, attitude of coaching staff regarding the student athlete's academic interests, and availability of tutors and academic counselors within the athletic department or university academic counseling center.

TIME DEMANDS

Being a student athlete in college requires the individual to divide his or her time between academic studies and athletics. The demands of being a college athlete are tremendous, especially at major universities. In Division I competition, particularly in the revenue-producing sports of basketball, baseball, soccer, and football, the academic and athletic time demands on the student athlete could add up to 70 or even 80 hours per week. Athletics-related activities, which could require as many as 40 hours per week, would include team meetings, taping, film sessions, conditioning, practice, games, and travel. In addition, the typical student spends approximately 35 hours per week attending classes, doing homework, working with tutors, and attending mandatory study tables, or supervised study sessions. This demanding schedule leaves little time for socializing or anything else.

It is very important for the college-bound student athlete to understand that the course work in college is considerably different and more difficult than course work in high school. It will require more time and effort to maintain the same grades. More academic accountability is placed on the student in college, and, generally, more intensive research and investigative analysis are the norm for most courses. Commitment and time management are keys to becoming a successful student while still coping with athletic demands. The individual must become the architect of his or her day, week, month, and semester, learning to balance time wisely. Workshops or seminars in time management can help students avoid the shock of being unprepared, which could lead to academic failure, loss of eligibility, loss of scholarships, and suspension from the team.

For some individuals, the demands of being a student and an athlete can be too great. Generally, the academic performance of the student athlete is sacrificed to meet the athletic demands of the coach. Also, unfortunately, some college faculty believe that student athletes, particularly Black student athletes, are not as intelligent or as academically competitive as the average student. Sometimes intentional or unintentional behavior or remarks on the part of instructors can have a negative impact on the student athlete's self-esteem and can adversely affect academic performance. Many college and university athletic departments have established academic networks to handle such problems. Academic counselors within the college athletic department are present to counsel and/or tutor athletes to help them improve in their course work. These counselors and tutors should be utilized when the student athlete experiences academic problems or unfair treatment by a member of the faculty.

GRADUATION RATES

There is widespread debate regarding the graduation rates of college athletes. Currently, approximately 56% of college athletes graduate within 5 years. However, the graduation rates for student athletes participating in NCAA Division I football and basketball are considerably lower, 47% and 39% respectively (Lederman, 1991). The reasons for low graduation rates are varied and complex. Media writers and social scientists are critical of athletic departments. They assert that "win at all costs" philosophies place too much pressure on student athletes, causing difficulty in the academic realm. While athletes must maintain at least a C average in 12 credit hours of course work per semester and make verifiable progress toward a specific degree in order to maintain their college eligibility, many are barely able to meet those academic requirements. Student athletes claim the time demands of their sports are too great and detract from their ability to perform academically. They complain that the "win at all costs" mentality that exists within the athletic department provides them with too little time for their studies (Chu, Segrave, & Becker, 1985).

Sometimes, coaches and academic counselors will place the athlete in unchallenging courses in order to offset academic difficulties and make it easier for the student athlete to remain eligible. These courses generally are selected randomly and do not lead toward the completion of a degree. Too often student athletes find themselves several credits short of graduation once their eligibility has expired.

Coaches are critical of their athletic departments and athletic boosters. They claim the intense pressure to produce winning programs compels them to recruit academically underprepared or scholastically marginal "blue chip" athletes who will help them win but who have little or no chance of graduating. Coaches are also critical of student athletes who refuse to attend class and who are not serious about their academic responsibilities. Lapchick (1989) estimates that 44% of minority athletes who compete in NCAA Division I basketball or football believe that they will be drafted and sign a professional contract. Some college athletes have candidly admitted they are not serious about their academics and are only in college to increase their chances of playing professionally. These student athletes do not attend class, and request enrollment in easy courses to maintain their eligibility. The unfortunate truth is only 1% of college athletes get to sign a professional sports contract. Generally, the student athlete would be much better off attending class, completing the degree requirements for graduation, and pursuing more practical employment. It is the responsibility of school counselors, teachers, and parents to inform student athletes about the traps of big-time college and professional sports, and to encourage them to make practical educational and life decisions.

Graduation rates vary at each school. The percentage of student athletes who graduate from a particular college or university is an accurate indication of that athletic department's level of commitment to academic excellence. High school prospects should avoid those schools whose athletic departments do not graduate their student athletes.

MYTHS AND STEREOTYPES

Myths and stereotypes create barriers to the academic success of college athletes. A recent study by Sailes (1991) revealed that many students and faculty members felt the athlete was not as competitive in the classroom as on the field. To the contrary, recent publication of graduation rates showed that athletes had similar grade point averages and slightly higher graduation rates than the average student (Norman, 1991). Knowing this, incoming student athletes should maintain confidence about their academic capabilities and not let any teasing or prejudice discourage them.

CONCLUSION

The decision to attend college is a serious one. Receiving an athletic scholarship to attend college is a privilege accorded less than 1% of the population. It should be regarded as an opportunity to establish higher priorities and to further one's goals. The process of selecting a college requires serious thought and consultation with experienced adults. Student athletes will be required to demonstrate dedication, discipline, commitment, and focus in order to be successful in college. A well-informed student athlete will have the greatest opportunity for a positive and beneficial college experience. School counselors and parents can play a major role in keeping student athletes informed and assisting them in the decision-making process.

References

Chu, D., Segrave, J., & Becker, B. (1985). *Sport and higher education*. Champaign, IL: Human Kinetics.

Crouse, J., & Trusheim, D. (1988). *The case against the SAT*. Chicago: University of Chicago Press.

Lapchick, R. (1989, April 20). *The Black athlete in intercollegiate sport*. Presentation at the Annual Conference of the American Alliance for Health, Physical Education, Recreation and Dance, Boston.

Lederman, D. (1991, March 27). College athletes graduate at higher rate than other students. *Chronicle of Higher Education*, pp. A1, A38–A44.

National Collegiate Athletic Association. (1991). *NCAA guide for the college-bound student-athlete*. Mission, KS: Author.

Norman, J. (1991, June 17). Graduation rate study spans half a decade. *USA Today*, p. 7C.

Sailes, G. A. (1990, May 12). The case against NCAA Proposition 48. *Indianapolis Recorder*, p. B-9.

Sailes, G. A. (1991, April 23). *An investigation of campus typecasts: The dumb jock stereotype and the myth of Black athlete superiority*. Paper presented at the national meeting of the American Alliance for Health, Physical Education, Recreation and Dance, San Francisco.

PART II

ATHLETICS AND SPECIAL ISSUES

CHAPTER 7

Counseling Athletes in Higher Education

WAYNE LANNING AND PETER TOYE

Counseling services for athletes in higher education receive a great deal of public scrutiny. A common myth in higher education, and in society in general, is that because athletes receive so much special attention they are the "privileged few" in colleges and universities. Little sympathy is generated for them (Lanning, 1982). Nevertheless, these athletes (and their counterparts in the high schools) are perhaps more in need of counseling services than their nonathlete counterparts, precisely because of their special status. This chapter will identify some of the issues that must be addressed in counseling with athletes in higher education. In addition, it will identify and discuss some of the special ethical difficulties that arise in counseling this population.

SPECIAL CONSIDERATIONS IN ATHLETIC COUNSELING IN HIGHER EDUCATION

Many people argue that athletes in higher education should be treated just as all other students are treated. Special treatment, they say, is not desirable, because it only serves to send athletes the message that they are special and/or privileged. We differ with that common assertion. If athletes are treated the same as all other students, then many of their needs are not going to be addressed. Typically, college athletes have counseling needs similar to those of their nonathlete peers, but in addition they have needs that are either unique to them or magnified by their positions as athletes. Counselors in higher education settings must be aware of and sensitive to those special needs if the athletes are to receive the optimum benefit from the services available.

Development of a Sense of Entitlement

The term *entitlement* can be defined as "that which I deserve by the nature of who I am." We all have beliefs about what we are entitled to based on our professional position, whether it is physician, teacher, counselor, politician, or clerk. When those beliefs develop into excessive and unrealistic attitudes, they can become problematic. Kriegman (1988) describes attitudes of excessive entitlement as involving "exaggerated ideas of what the person has a right to do" (p. 6). He further postulates that people possessing such excessive attitudes reflect them with beliefs such as:

> "The world owes me a living. I should always be approved of. I can do anything I want. My desires and needs are the most important thing in life. I should be catered to." They may make it plain that they consider themselves charming and good looking. It is usual to label such people arrogant, smug, selfish, demanding, pretentious. (p. 6)

If we apply these attitudes to athletics, examples of an athlete's exaggerated sense of entitlement become apparent. Such attitudes may manifest themselves in an athlete's belief that "I am what I do, and if I do it well, I can deserve special treatment." Such a belief develops over many years of continued reinforcement by parents, coaches, peers, and fans, and certainly may continue in college. By the time a young athlete reaches a postsecondary institution, he or she may fully expect preferential treatment and, in many cases, receive it. Such treatment only provides further reinforcement for the dysfunctional attitude that "the world owes me a living."

Although an excessive sense of entitlement may initially limit an individual's full development academically, socially, and emotionally, most college athletes soon realize that regardless of what they were told in the recruiting process, the treatment they believe they deserve and the treatment they actually receive are two different things. Counseling can be very beneficial at this point to help student athletes adjust to a new environment and to the realization that they may not be as "special" as they were in high school.

Significant problems arise for those student athletes who persist in the belief that because they are athletes they are entitled to special treatment academically, socially, legally, and athletically. They maintain these beliefs and expectations because they have experienced such entitlements in the past and fully expect them to continue. Student athletes with such beliefs might expect to be given better grades than their performance actually warrants. They might look for special treatment from the nonathlete population on campus, such as sexual favors or free admission to parties. Individuals with an overdeveloped sense of entitlement also often do not expect to be held accountable for illegal activities both on and off campus; they assume the law does not apply to them. Particularly outstanding athletes might think they are entitled to decrease their practice attendance and effort. It is imperative that coaches and counselors alike identify student athletes with such attitudes and work closely with them. Colleges and universities have only a short period of time to intervene and help change these attitudes before a young person is forced to leave school for academic, social, legal, or athletics-related reasons.

Counseling interventions should focus on the dysfunctional aspects of an excessive sense of entitlement and the probable consequences of maintaining such an attitude (e.g., failing school, incarceration). It is important to confront and challenge these firmly entrenched attitudes, with the ultimate goal being to assist the student athlete in developing a more realistic view of the world before it is too late.

Peer Group Difficulties

Student athletes do not relate to others as "just another student," because they are not typical students. Most of them are involved in their sport for great quantities of time during the entire school year. As a result, most of their peer relationships are formed with fellow athletes, frequently those involved in the same sport. Training tables, study tables, and weight rooms are reserved for athletes, and therefore most of their social contact is with other athletes.

The world of athletics contains subcultures of people who have similar backgrounds, interests, and needs, and peer relationships are based upon the rules of the specific subculture within which they develop. In general, though, most athlete peer groups place a higher premium on competitiveness than do nonathlete peer groups. Successful athletes have thrived on fierce competition most of their lives, even in their relationships with their closest peers. They have placed the goals of the sport above the types of goals nonathletes might focus on. Such prioritizing lends itself to peculiar dynamics and problems in relationships among athletes. "When the going gets tough, the tough get going" is a motto that still hangs on the walls of many locker rooms in athletic departments. It is better to be tough than tender. Opposition is to be overcome rather than understood and accommodated. In peer group relations those rules lead to a prohibition against being personally vulnerable or "soft."

Therefore, athletes have a special need to understand that the world outside of athletics contains additional elements in personal relationships and that those elements are not forbidden. When they do learn to develop relationships outside of athletics, athletes are further challenged to understand and manage the tensions that might result from having peer relationships in two different worlds. That which is so highly valued in the world of athletics is not the basis for satisfying relationships with peers outside of athletics.

Counselors in higher education settings would be wise to consider that many of the interpersonal difficulties athletes have can be traced to the competitive standards entrenched in most of their social interactions. Guided by that awareness, the counselor can better understand that what appears to be a devastating cruelty in an athletic relationship may not be seen as such by the athlete. The counselor who understands the unique socialization process in athlete peer groups is also better equipped to help the athlete develop more varied interpersonal skills.

Career Choice Problems

Perhaps the most difficulty for athletes lies in the choices they make for careers. Nearly every athlete in the revenue-producing sports dreams of being a professional athlete and making a huge salary. Media accounts of average salaries for athletes provide the "carrot on the stick" for young athletes to follow. Popular television advertisements implore youngsters to "be like Mike" by wearing the same kind of shoes and clothes and even drinking the same beverages. The message is that all children should aspire to attain the level of athletic excellence that their media-created heros have attained. But fewer than 2% of college athletes ever sign professional contracts to play their sport (Lee, 1983). That leaves over 98% who have to make decisions about some meaningful and gainful employment in the non-athletic world. Most, sadly, are unprepared to make those decisions.

Career choice is now considered a process rather than an event (O'Hare, 1987). Most college-age students will need to make a number of major career shifts in their lifetimes. Even the few who do compete professionally have a very short productive athletic life span (Petitpas & Champagne, 1988). They, too, must still decide what to do with their lives when the playing days are over. Many nonathlete students go to college with no idea of what they want to do upon completion, but all acknowledge that a productive job is the goal toward which they work. Athletes are typically blinded to all possibilities except that of future athletic excellence. In higher education, this appears to be a greater problem for male athletes than for female athletes (Blann, 1985). Programs need to be developed for athletes that help them get a realistic view of their future and then teach them the skills necessary to make the career decisions that face them. Those programs must be endorsed and promoted by the coaches. Otherwise, student athletes will view them as just another activity to be tolerated, rather than as one of value. The report of the Knight Foundation Commission on Intercollegiate Athletics (1991) addresses the student athlete when it states:

> We plead with you to understand that—unless you are one of the remarkably talented and very lucky—when your athletic ability has expired your playing days are over. Your task, even if you are one of the fortunate few, is to prepare yourself for the years and decades that stretch ahead of you beyond college. (p. 28)

Conditional Acceptance

Self-esteem is a highly popular but ill-defined construct in today's educational environment. Typically it means the sum total of feelings one has about himself or herself in all aspects of life (Newman & Newman, 1987). Increasing self-esteem, therefore, involves increasing an individual's ability to be accepting of whatever he or she is. Self-esteem may be based on one's view of self more than on the real self, and self-perception is often contextual (Rosenberg, 1979). Many people learn to establish and maintain a sense of worth or self-esteem by performing well in areas that they learn are valued and rewarded. A person who learns to value the acquisition of great wealth may become driven to pursue that singular goal throughout life. One who learns to value the acquisition of new knowledge may well pursue only that as a lifelong goal. And one who learns to value athletic excellence, and who is highly rewarded for it, soon learns to seek personal worth or self-esteem almost solely by means of athletic performance. Anyone whose self-esteem is based upon a primary ability struggles when that ability or attribute is lost or jeopardized. However, many people learn to base their self-worth on a variety of roles and abilities, so that when one is lost they can focus on other roles to regain their sense of self-worth. Successful athletes in higher education frequently have been rewarded for the singular attribute of athletic prowess, or at least that is the only one they have noticed. When their athletic abilities are diminished or removed through injury or loss of eligibility, those athletes are shaken. They are not aware of alternative roles through which they can build self-worth. Therefore, counseling programs that seek to meet the special needs of athletes must help athletes to establish and maintain alternative bases for personal success.

Counseling Injured Athletes

The importance of providing counseling services to injured athletes has been consistently documented in the literature (Andersen & Williams, 1988; Heyman, 1987; May & Sieb, 1987). Injury, or the threat of injury, is certainly a real part of every competitive athlete's existence. Injuries can be separated into three categories: minor (requiring little time away from the sport), major (requiring significant time away from competition), and severe (career-ending). We will focus, here, on counseling athletes with major and severe injuries, which we will refer to collectively as "serious" injuries.

Counseling seriously injured athletes becomes more problematic when the bulk of the individual's identity, and the primary source of self-esteem, has been centered in athletic performance. It is a grave error in judgment to underestimate the importance of athletic performance to athletes who have been reinforced for little else throughout their lives. To the athletes who find serious injury most traumatic, sport is not "just a game" any more than art is "just drawing" or professional dance is "just dancing." Intercollegiate competition is a way of life for many young men and women. Sensitivity to the psychological implications of the injury is paramount if a meaningful relationship is to develop between counselor and client. To an athlete whose career is terminated due to injury, the loss may be as traumatic as a sculptor's loss of her hands or a dancer's loss of his feet.

Serious injury can mark the death of a career. The Kubler-Ross (1969) model provides a theoretical framework within which to explain the process of grieving such a death. Kubler-Ross's five-stage model has previously been utilized for counseling professional athletes whose careers have been terminated due to retirement (Wolff & Lester, 1989), and also provides a functional framework for counseling athletes who have sustained serious, career-threatening injuries. The five stages described by Kubler-Ross are denial, anger, bargaining, depression, and acceptance.

The primary objective for counseling injured athletes is basically two-fold. First, the athlete must work through the grief and learn to accept the realities of the injury. Second, the athlete's self-awareness must be expanded so that he or she can envision options beyond the narrow scope of competitive sports. This is no easy task given the glamour and life-style that may have been associated with previous athletic involvement.

ETHICAL DIFFICULTIES AND CONSIDERATIONS IN COUNSELING ATHLETES IN HIGHER EDUCATION

Dealing With Coaches

To better understand the ethical issues involved in the professional relationship between an athlete's counselor and coach, a brief review of a college coach's reality is in order. The fact that winning is the most important thing in college sports is news only to the naive. Coakley (1990) recognized the brutal truth when he stated that "winning is the most important, if not the only criterion used to determine if coaches are successful" (p. 165). Despite the criticism regarding graduation rates and academic performance of student athletes by groups like the Knight Foundation Commission (1991) and the United States Senate ("McMillen Introduces," 1991), little has yet been done to alter the stark coaching reality of "win or walk."

As a response to the overbearing pressure to win, coaches may desire significant control over all phases of their athletes' lives (Coakley, 1990). The coach's desire to know everything about the athletes can create unique tensions between a coach and the counselor working with the athletes. Friction can develop if the coach feels the counselor is "withholding vital information" relative to the athlete, but that friction is much more the coach's issue than the counselor's. The positions of both the American Counseling Association (ACA) and the National Association of Academic Advisors for Athletics (N4A) are clear regarding confidentiality. The ACA Code of Ethics compels a counselor to maintain confidentiality unless the client is a clear danger to self or others (Corey, Corey, & Callanan, 1988). Concomitantly, the N4A Code of Ethics (1989) requires the membership to "respect privacy and counselor confidentiality in disclosing information to the coaches or faculty" (p. 4). Furthermore, the N4A Code succinctly states that the counselor's primary obligation is to the student athlete and not to the program. This is a very important distinction, because many times what is in the best interest of the individual may not be in the best interest of the specific program. For example, suppose a counselor is working with a male basketball player during fall semester. At the end of November the young man tells the counselor that he has decided to stay home after Christmas. The athlete is a key player around whom the team has been built, and he refuses to tell the coach out of fear of retaliation. Knowing that the shock of the athlete's decision will bring chaos to the program, the counselor still has no choice but to maintain confidentiality, regardless of the ensuing furor.

Counselors of student athletes must explain the ethical obligations of confidentiality to coaches so that expectations are clearly understood. At times the coaches themselves will be the athlete's primary problem, and such revelations must be protected for obvious reasons.

It is easy for counselors who work in athletics departments to lose their identity as counselors and assume the role of coaches. Of course, this transformation is a mistake. Coaches are not counselors, and for good reason. A coach's primary concern is the team; a counselor's primary concern must be the individual. This separation is most imperative as it relates to the application of disciplinary sanctions against individual student athletes who have violated team rules. For a counselor to be involved in the punishment of athletes undermines the maintenance of the nonjudgmental attitude that is so critical in the counseling relationship. Student athletes must be allowed the freedom to choose without fear of either retribution by the counselor or the breaking of confidentiality to a coach. Otherwise, the counselor becomes little more than a departmental snitch who will never be trusted by the very population he or she is expected to serve. Once trust is destroyed, it may be impossible for the counselor to ever restore it at that institution. Hence, the counselor is in the precarious position of having to maintain credibility with both the athletes and the coaches.

Working With Nonvolunteer Clients

Client resistance to counseling is a common occurrence and will manifest itself in a variety of forms, including silence, verbosity, and emotional display (Otani, 1989). Nonvolunteer student-athlete clients usually have been referred by the coach for reasons such as suspicion of drug abuse, unexplained behavioral changes, and the ever-popular "poor attitude." The coach might also require the student athlete to maintain a weekly appointment with a counselor so that academic progress can be more closely monitored.

Initially, tension may be high in the sessions with nonvoluntary clients, but most student athletes soon realize that the counselor is on their side, and from that realization trust will soon follow. This is precisely why the counselor must be an advocate for the student athlete and not for the program. At the same time, the counselor should have a working, nonadversarial relationship with the coach, so that the referral process can take place. A coach should not be expected to diagnose psychological problems, but should be expected to know when something is amiss with a young person under his or her supervision, and to refer accordingly. Generally, coaches are good evaluators of behavior and can play a critical role in providing the information required for early intervention with an athlete in need.

The counselor may insist on mandatory attendance at regularly scheduled sessions. Even though client autonomy is a major goal of counseling, not all young people come to college with that ideal perspective in place. With some individuals who present significant learning or behavioral difficulties, we have about a year to either help them find a more effective way of managing their lives or help them pack their bags. Naturally, many of these student athletes do not seek the help of a counselor because it is not their style. Coaches can provide great assistance in motivating this type of nonvolunteer client to honor appointment times. Consequences regarding missed appointments must be clearly spelled out to the student athlete, so that the counselor does not become the disciplinarian when the client misses an appointment.

Dual Roles of Counselors

Problems may arise for the athletic counselor who also has administrative duties in an athletic department. At some institutions, the director of athletic counseling may also have the title of assistant or associate athletic director, and may be expected to make the image of the entire athletic program a primary concern. This dual role of counselor/administrator can frequently create a conflict of interest between what is best for a given individual and what is best for the program. Such conflict can, however, be reconciled. The position of athletic counselor/administrator is no different from that of counselor/administrator at a university counseling center. Most university counseling center directors are expected to administer their unit in a manner consistent with the overall mission of the university while still maintaining a client caseload.

Ethically, there is little major conflict between a professional's obligations as a counselor and his or her obligations as an administrator. Politically, however, there may be a great deal of difference. A counselor may be working with a student athlete who is involved in an activity that embarrasses the entire university. Because of confidentiality considerations, the counselor may be unable to do anything about it. Conflict exists where the administrative role requires that the student be removed from the program but the counselor role demands continued work with the student. In such situations, the integrity of the counseling relationship must take precedence.

If a significant, persistent conflict of interest develops, a professional may be forced to choose between counseling and administration. Sometimes what is best for the student athlete may not be best for the program, and vice versa. When the program begins taking priority over the client, the choice has already been made.

CONCLUSION

Athletes in higher education have all of the needs that nonathletes have, but in addition they have many needs unique to their status as student athletes. Institutions of higher education are remiss if they do not develop counseling and other support services that address these needs of the student athlete. Special counseling offices do not necessarily have to be established to work specifically with student athletes. Many institutions already have established services for the entire student population. However, many of those offices are not staffed with counselors who have an understanding of the special needs of the student athlete. In fact, many counselors and student personnel workers adamantly refuse to consider treating student athletes as different, because they object to the attitude of entitlement discussed earlier. Nevertheless, if counselors are to respond to each student as someone with individual needs, it is imperative that student athletes be considered for the individual needs they have as members of that athlete subgroup.

Difficulties arise when a counselor's personal issues with college athletics interfere with the counseling intervention. A patronizing or condescending attitude, for instance, can impede the development of a meaningful counseling relationship. Of course, this problem is not unique to counseling with student athletes, and such counselor attitudes must be addressed when working with any client population. When a counselor finds himself or herself to be in an ethically compromising situation, referral should be considered.

The athletic counselor can draw upon many resources within the institution to provide better assistance to the student athlete. Many student personnel offices, such as the dean of students, residence life, international programs, career centers, campus ministry, and the counseling center, are staffed by trained professionals who can be of assistance in specific situations. The effective professional counselor within an athletic department will be aware of the support upon which he or she can draw in order to provide the best services to student athletes.

References

Andersen, M., & Williams, J. (1988). A model of stress and athletic injury: Prediction and prevention. *Journal of Sport and Exercise Physiology, 10,* 294–306.

Blann, F. W. (1985). The relationship of students' competitive level of participation in inter-collegiate athletics and their ability to formulate mature educational and career plans. *Journal of College Student Personnel, 26,* 115–118.

Coakley, J. (1990). *Sport in society* (4th ed.). St. Louis: Times.

Corey, C., Corey, M., & Callanan, P. (1988). *Issues and ethics in the helping professions* (3rd ed.). Pacific Grove, CA: Brooks/Cole.

Heyman, S. (1987). Counseling and psychotherapy with athletes: Special considerations. In J. R. May & M. J. Askern (Eds.), *Sport psychology* (pp. 135–156). New York: PMA.

Knight Foundation Commission on Intercollegiate Athletics. (1991). *Keeping faith with the student-athlete: A new model for intercollegiate athletics.* Charlotte, NC: Commission on Intercollegiate Athletics.

Kriegman, G. (1988). Entitlement attitudes: Psychological and therapeutic implications. In V. D. Volkan & T. C. Rodgers (Eds.), *Attitudes of entitlement* (pp. 1–22). Charlottesville, VA: University Press.

Kubler-Ross, E. (1969). *On death and dying.* London: MacMillan.

Lanning, W. (1982). The privileged few: Special counseling needs of athletes. *Journal of Sport Psychology, 4,* 19–23.

Lee, C. C. (1983). An investigation of the athletic career expectations of high school athletes. *The Personnel and Guidance Journal, 61,* 544–547.

May, J., & Sieb, G. (1987). Athletic injuries: Psychological factors in the onset, sequelae, rehabilitation, and prevention. In J. R. May & M. J. Askern (Eds.), *Sport psychology* (pp. 157–185). New York: PMA.

McMillen introduces athletics reform act. (1991, July 31). *NCAA News,* pp. 1, 3.

National Association of Academic Advisors for Athletics Code of Ethics. (1989, Fall). *Academic Athletic Journal,* pp. 1–5.

Newman, B. M., & Newman, P. R. (1987). *Development through life: A psychological approach* (4th ed.). Pacific Grove, CA: Brooks/Cole.

O'Hare, M. M. (1987). Career decision-making models: Espoused theory versus theory-in-use. *Journal of Counseling and Development, 65,* 301–303.

Otani, A. (1989). Client resistance in counseling: Its theoretical rationale and taxonomic classification. *Journal of Counseling and Development, 67,* 458–461.

Petitpas, A., & Champagne, D. E. (1988). Developmental programming for intercollegiate athletes. *Journal of College Student Development, 29,* 454–460.

Rosenberg, M. (1979). *Conceiving the self.* New York: Basic Books.

Wolff, R., & Lester, D. (1989). A theoretical basis for counseling the retired professional athlete. *Psychological Reports, 64,* 1043–1046.

CHAPTER 8

Problem Solving and Decision Making: Life Skills for Student Athletes

J. SCOTT HINKLE

Sports and athletics are growing exponentially in the United States. Increases in leisure time and the sensationalism of the sports world are but two of the numerous factors responsible for captivating even the youngest athlete. Sports will continue to be a dominant force well into the 21st century. As a result, student athletes will need assistance in many human service areas. For example, Allen (1988) has successfully used classroom instruction to teach athletes self-improvement skills. Despite such efforts and those mentioned in chapter 7, the professionalization of sports and the increased involvement of sanctioning bodies will lead to problems related to sports performance for many student athletes. The popular press and television sports broadcasters describe the plight of athletes on a daily basis. Common difficulties range from conflicts with peers and authority figures to drug abuse and addiction. In addition, many athletes are experiencing personal problems of a clinical nature, including significant levels of stress (Bergandi & Wittig, 1984; Lederman, 1988) caused by inadequate problem-solving and decision-making skills.

An informal survey of books concerning sports and psychology has revealed a plethora of information on performance enhancement, strategies for motivating athletes, and sports competition and aggression. However, there is a modicum of information and programs regarding the development of life skills such as problem solving among athletes. Many athletes' lives are rigidly structured by others. They may fear making their own decisions or exhibit faulty decision-making styles (Crace, 1989). Moreover, many major life decisions are made for student athletes; subsequently, they do not feel that universities and coaches have prepared them well for life (Boone & Walker, 1987). Some athletes tend to accept dominant normative values and life-styles rather than explore their own alternatives (Petitpas & Champagne, 1988; Schafer, 1971), while others are overprotected (Lanning, 1982).

Many athletes see no need to examine their own behavior. They may view themselves as having a solid identity and leading a busy but regulated life (Petitpas & Champagne, 1988). If responsibility for problem solving and goal setting can be shifted from the university and coach to the athlete (Chartrand & Lent, 1987), these young people ultimately will be much better served.

Approximately 25% of student athletes want help for their difficulties, but only about 5% seek assistance from an external source. People working with athletes need to be cognizant of their need for help and provide the coping-skills training necessary for them to successfully negotiate trouble-some life events (Bunker & McGuire, 1985). Not surprisingly, 70% of the general student athlete population have reported a need to obtain assistance from their coach (Selby, Weinstein, & Bird, 1990). Therefore, coping-skills training, including problem solving, can be beneficial for coaches as well as student athletes. This chapter will focus on the development of a problem-solving model that can be utilized by athletes, coaches, and others involved with student athletes. Use of this model can make the transfer of sports-related skills to life skills more effective and efficient.

LIFE SKILLS FOR ATHLETES

As with many aspects of life, athletics involves fact and fantasy, myth and reality. Many young athletes are enamored with the recognition, popularity, and potential fame and fortune associated with a very small percentage of sports figures. Athletes are constantly caught in a struggle to balance realistic life expectations and idealistic goals (Smallman, Sowa, & Young, 1991). Not only must they satisfy themselves, but athletes also feel they must satisfy parents, peers, and coaches. In this respect, coaches and others involved with athletes need to humanize sports (Butt, 1987).

Although athletes learn many skills in their selected sports, many never learn to extrapolate or transfer these skills, or skill components, to other areas of life. It is extremely important for sports program developers and those responsible for student athletes to infuse life-skills development into athletics. Rather than contributing to the "little league syndrome," or insisting that winning is everything, parents, coaches, and athletic departments can assist athletes in the development of important life skills such as problem solving and decision making. This is a much easier task when sports-related skills are utilized to enhance life skills.

Exactly how people solve problems is unknown (Heppner, 1978). However, it is important to note that most athletes become reasonably good problem solvers within the context of their sports. Just as the athlete transfers strenuous physical and mental training and practice to competitive situations, so must the athlete learn to transfer effective sports-related skills to his or her personal life. In much the same way, internal standards regarding sports can be generalized to nonsport life situations. However, making decisions becomes difficult for many student athletes when the problematic event occurs outside of the parameters of sport. Thus, athletes will benefit from fundamental problem-solving approaches that incorporate behaviors from the realm of athletics.

A PROBLEM-SOLVING MODEL FOR ATHLETES

When significant costs and risks are involved, decisions can have dramatic effects on people's lives (Janis & Mann, 1977). Two fundamentals of good decision making are maximizing gains and minimizing losses. Gains and losses might be manifested in the person's life-style or security level, or in a variety of psychological, social, and environmental factors and conditions (Vacc & Loesch, 1987).

No single formula can account for all the theoretical variables associated with personal problem solving. There are a number of scientific strategies concerning decision making and problem solving; some even include complicated mathematical formulas and computer simulations (Heppner, 1978). Others divide the process into definable stages (e.g., D'Zurilla & Goldfried, 1971). Of these, the approach of Krumboltz, Mitchell, and Jones (1978), utilized in career choice, can be practically applied to athletics. This approach, based on social learning theory, focuses on four variables: (a) genetic endowment, (b) environmental conditions, (c) learning experiences, and (d) task approach skills. The author has included an additional variable germane to athletes: psychological resources. The current model is a problem-solving and decision-making strategy circumscribed in a *discover, uncover, recover* continuum that can be easily utilized by athletes as well as by sports counselors, athletic administrators, student affairs personnel, faculty, and parents. This problem-solving continuum also includes goal setting, exploring alternatives, decision making, and ultimately the transfer of sports skills to life skills (see Figure 1).

In the *discovery* phase, the first phase of the problem-solving process, the athlete identifies variables that are associated with the problematic event. Also in this first stage, the athlete labels and qualifies troublesome situations. To gain an accurate understanding of the problem, student athletes must gather facts and information so that vague concepts can be operationalized (Heppner, 1978). In addition, self-exploration experiences can help the individual come up with meaningful explanations for the problem (Petitpas & Champagne, 1988). This process may include such counseling techniques as reflecting, summarizing, interpreting, and probing (Heppner, 1978). Other counseling techniques (i.e., Gestalt, Transactional Analysis, Rational Emo-

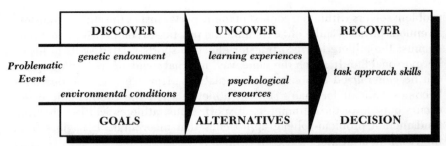

Figure 1. Problem-Solving Model for Student Athletes

tive Therapy) may also be used to assist with gathering data during the discovery stage. The initial discovery component also includes an evaluation of any existing innate or genetic factors and environmental conditions.

In general, innate physical and mental strengths should be realistically assessed. Although this can be accomplished in a formal manner, a simple review of the student athlete's major life events may be all that is necessary. Specifically, for example, an athlete may become aware of long-term personal issues and beliefs regarding physical appearance (i.e., too tall, too big, too awkward) by simply identifying the types of events that seem to interfere with effective day-to-day problem solving. Recognizing such concerns helps the athlete discover other personal information, process it, and incorporate it into the decision-making scheme.

Goals and objectives are an integral part of the discovery component. Potential goals should be ranked in some meaningful and logical order. Athletes constantly engage in setting such priorities within the sports domain. For example, athletes will decide if they are ready to challenge for the championship, place in their own category, or simply have a good performance. Athletes set such goals on a daily basis, and these goal-setting procedures need to be effectively transferred to problem solving in general. Objectives, or successive approximations of the goal, are often encountered within sports. Likewise, mini-goals or objectives can be transferred to problem-solving situations outside of sports.

The *uncovering* phase includes an examination of personal factors such as past learning experiences and psychological resources. From a psychological perspective, this component of the current model focuses on underlying motivations for behavior and on its consequences. Uncovering the psychological themes associated with particular past learning experiences can eventually result in new motivations for behavior change. To illustrate, an athlete may find that an avoidant behavior problem is possibly related to issues with authority figures that have developed from long-standing parent-child difficulties. Once this information has been uncovered, the athlete may have a new meaning attribution for the avoidance, and may eventually recover from the difficulty as well as learn to apply this data to the problem-solving process.

Evaluating alternatives and establishing mental scenarios for the various options is integral to the uncovering component of this model. Heppner (1978) has suggested that the generation of alternatives should be goal directed. In sports events, athletes are often faced with situations in which they must choose from among several alternatives. With some "practice," they can transfer this experience to their life skills repertoire. Training and practice will improve the quality of alternatives generated (Dixon, Heppner, Petersen, & Ronning, 1979). Selection of alternatives is also indirectly affected by such factors as genetic endowment, special abilities, environmental conditions, past learning experiences, and psychological resources.

The *recovery* phase finalizes the problem-solving process. In this stage, task approach skills are utilized to help the athlete reach a decision that supports personal growth and adds to the repertoire of life skills. At this final stage in the problem-solving process, the athlete has moved from a state of uncertainty to a state of certainty. The recovery phase provides the athlete with a mechanism to apply personal information gathered during the discovery and uncovering stages. Once personal information has been brought to the surface, the athlete is prepared to finish the process by "putting all the pieces of the puzzle together." Finally the student athlete reaches a solution that maximizes the number of positive consequences and minimizes the negative ones.

Genetic Endowment

According to Vacc & Loesch (1987), the term "genetic endowment" refers to such factors as gender, special abilities, ethnicity, and intelligence. Since these variables are typically indirect factors in the problem-solving process, they are often overlooked. However, attention to sex bias (see chapter 10), physical limitations, racial and ethnic issues, and academic and intellectual deficits can significantly benefit the student athlete as he or she learns to solve life problems. Athletes focusing on problematic areas within their respective sports are aware of physical strengths and weaknesses; they use this information on a daily basis during training and practice. Once identified or discovered, such awareness may also be applied to problem solving outside of sports.

To further illustrate, one athlete at the NCAA Division II level experienced chronic academic problems that jeopardized his collegiate sports career. When he discovered he had minimized the importance of classroom activities since middle school, the difficulty was reframed. He realized he possessed the inherent intelligence necessary for academic success, and that he simply had never applied himself in academics as he had in sports. When the difficulty was presented as a new challenge and related issues were uncovered, this individual was able to put the "student" back into his role of student athlete.

Environmental Conditions

Social circumstances within sports are important environmental factors that require close assessment by athletes. Similarly, social expectations and the need for approval and support emerge as significant factors in other areas of life as well. Social facilitation and group compliance, along with potential susceptibility to influence from others, should be considered as elements in the problem-solving process. Student athletes are often caught in peer struggles on their teams. Competing for positions or even for a chance to play may create extremely difficult social conditions. However, athletic cultures have systems for solving such problems. For instance, team members may establish an acceptable hierarchical order and adhere to it, or an athlete may be placed in a different playing position or role. Many student athletes become very adept at identifying the nature of the environmental situation and acting upon it. When confronted with a significant problem seperate from sports, a student athlete can use the same skills to examine environmental data or conditions. For example, problem solving can be affected socially by interpersonal role conflicts. Athletes often assume the roles of boyfriend, girlfriend, husband, wife, mother, and father, as well as student. When these roles are uncovered, the athlete may be better able to comprehend problematic circumstances and past experiences.

Learning Experiences

Another important variable in the problem-solving process is the utilization of past experiences (Schultz, 1960; Skinner, 1974). Learning experiences outside of sports might consist of formal training, educational experiences, and trial-and-error learning. Negative past experiences have been reported to elicit incompatible or inhibiting behavior that interferes with the task of problem solving (Shultz, 1960). Student athletes can learn to effectively apply both positive and negative past experiences, once those experiences are identified and their relationship to the problem assessed.

Athletes need to determine what information is needed, who possesses it, and how it can be obtained and integrated into the process of solving problems (Janis & Mann, 1977). To do this efficiently, student athletes need to develop an information-processing orientation to examine various available options (Janis & Mann, 1977) and past learning experiences. The ability to weigh the probable costs and risks of various alternatives is crucial. Again, athletes do this often in training and in competition and need to transfer this skill to other areas. Hence, the total range of sport and life learning experiences and their application to particular life problems can potentially be quite beneficial.

Psychological Resources

The process of making a decision can be stressful. To develop and adhere to a plan of action, accept some degree of risk, and minimize serious losses (Janis & Mann, 1977), athletes must be able to tap into psychological resources. Such resources may be internal or external. Examples of external resources include student counseling services, athletic assistance programs, and career planning and placement centers.

Any client will solve problems more effectively if he or she can access internal psychological resources. Although many student athletes are psychologically stressed from time to time (Lanning, 1982; Lederman, 1988), they also have personal traits and abilities that can serve them quite well during sports participation. These may include the ability to use self-statements to establish internal states and feelings (Heppner, 1978), confidence in personal competency (Heppner & Petersen, 1982), ability to deal with delay of gratification, and overall coping skills. The degree of personal control, including the capacity to deliberate about one's behavior and strategies for change, is also important (Heppner & Petersen, 1982). Athletes can use these various psychological resources in other arenas as well. Emotional adjustments used in sports competition can be discovered, uncovered, and applied to the recovery from a problematic situation.

Task Approach Skills

Task approach skills utilized in sports also can be generalized or transferred to areas outside the realm of sports to aid student athletes in problem solving. For example, training habits, cognitive processes, clarification of personal values, and evaluation of performance standards are skills that are often highly developed through participation in athletics. All of these are fundamental to effective problem solving. The problematic situation should not be avoided or acted on impulsively (Heppner, 1978), but rather it should be solved in a systematic fashion (Heppner & Petersen, 1982). Athletes should be encouraged to apply sports-related training habits and cognitive strategies to other areas of life.

CASE EXAMPLE

Harmon is a freshman baseball player, on scholarship at a major southeastern college whose team has recently competed in the College World Series. Harmon presented with several distressing problems and life issues. He had moved from the northwest to attend college, leaving behind his family and girlfriend. Harmon had initially preferred not to attend school so far from home. However, he rejected scholarship offers to play baseball in his home state because his parents strongly encouraged him to attend the southeastern college that would most likely contend for the national title in baseball. It was after many unsuccessful debates with his parents that Harmon accepted the out-of-state scholarship, moved across the country, and left his girlfriend behind. To make matters worse, financial constraints would only allow him to visit his family and girlfriend once during the entire academic year.

When Harmon came to the college counseling center, he was assigned to a counselor who had personal experience with sports and past involvement with athletic teams. The sports counselor (SC) implemented the discovery, uncovering, and recovery model by initiating the discovery phase in the first counseling session. Events that led to Harmon's current circumstances were identified within the context of his special abilities and environmental conditions. (In this case genetic endowment per se did not appear to be relevant; however, Harmon reported that he was an exceptional batter and baserunner.) Harmon was experiencing ongoing, long-term conflict with his parents and a sense of loss related to being away from his girlfriend. In the following two sessions, Harmon and the SC identified the various issues related to the problem and established initial goals.

Next, the SC entered an uncovering phase with Harmon that revealed anger toward his parents, lack of assertiveness skills, and mild depression due to the loss of his girlfriend. Past learning experiences related to the problem included an inability to speak up for himself and countless situations in which he had suppressed the expression of his feelings. The SC guided Harmon in listing psychological skills he used in sports and assisted him in effectively transferring and applying those skills to his personal crisis. Over the next few sessions, they discussed alternative behaviors, and Harmon was able to consider solving his delemma.

The recovery phase of the problem-solving process included transferring additional task approach skills he had learned in sports and integrating them with those learned in counseling. Harmon realized in a few weeks that he had many baseball-related problem-solving skills that could be applied to his personal life situation. For example, Harmon revealed his successful mental techniques for dealing with difficult sports fans at games. He also reported successfully refocusing his anger into intense concentration while playing, and freely sharing his emotions while at games. With renewed self-confidence, Harmon eventually decided to confront his parents about his decision to transfer to his home state to attend college and became engaged to his girlfriend. One year later, Harmon had married, and he and his wife returned to the southeastern college. He played baseball and earned his degree in business administration. His decision to return was the result of his negotiating with his parents, obtaining stability in his intimate relationship, and transferring sports skills to successful problem solving.

CONCLUSION

Congruence in one life role will generally influence other life roles (Crace, 1989). However, deficits in the quality of life are generally not satisfied through superficial involvement in sports. Sports in and out of itself will not compensate for deprivations in one's personal life (Spreitzer & Snyder, 1989). Thus, athletes need training and guidance in transferring effective sports-related skills to life skills. The model in this chapter is a simple and effective strategy for teaching athletes, coaches, and others about efficient problem solving within an athletic context. Only when student athletes are counseled in such a humanistic manner will they be able to meet their full potential.

The discovery, uncovering, and recovery model utilizes genetic and environmental factors that influence problem solving. Positive and negative learning experiences and existing psychological resources are reviewed for their impact on the problem. Finally, task approach skills that affect eventual decision making are assessed and extrapolated to nonsports situations. This model can help student athletes identify existing sports skills and apply them to other areas of life. It is a strength-versus-deficit model that explores existing knowledge and skills and develops them in an inviting manner for use outside of sports. As with any problem-solving model, the discover, uncover, and recover model will be refined with each practical application and with further empirical research.

References

Allen, T. W. (1988). The cognitive bases of peak performance: A classroom intervention with student-athletes. *Journal of Counseling and Development, 67*, 202–204.

Bergandi, T. A., & Wittig, A. F. (1984). Availability of and attitudes toward counseling services for the college athlete. *Journal of College Student Personnel, 25*, 557–558.

Boone, J. N., & Walker, H., Jr. (1987, February). *Ungraduated college athletes: Stereotype and reality.* Paper presented at the annual meeting of the Association for the Study of Higher Education, San Diego.

Bunker, L. K., & McGuire, R. T. (1985). Give sport psychology to sport. In L. K. Bunker, R. J. Rotella, & A. S. Reilly (Eds.), *Sport psychology* (pp. 3–14). Ann Arbor, MI: McNaughton & Gunn.

Butt, D. S. (1987). *Psychology of sport.* New York: Van Nostrand Reinhold.

Chartrand, J. M., & Lent, R. W. (1987). Sports counseling: Enhancing the development of the athlete. *Journal of Counseling and Development, 66*, 164–167.

Crace, R. K. (1989, March). Career development of the amateur and professional athlete using the life-role counseling model. In J. S. Hinkle (Chair), *Sport psychology: Perspectives on sports counseling.* Symposium conducted at the annual meeting of the Southeastern Psychological Association, Washington, DC.

Dixon, D. N., Heppner, P. P., Petersen, C. H., & Ronning, R. R. (1979). Problem-solving workshop training. *Journal of Counseling Psychology, 26*, 133–139.

D'Zurilla, T. J., & Goldfried, M. R. (1971). Problem-solving and behavior modification. *Journal of Abnormal Psychology, 78*, 107–126.

Heppner, P. P. (1978). A review of the problem-solving literature and its relationship to the counseling process. *Journal of Counseling Psychology, 25*, 366–375.

Heppner, P. P., & Petersen, C. H. (1982). The development and implications of a personal problem-solving inventory. *Journal of Counseling Psychology, 29*, 66–75.

Janis, I. L., & Mann, L. (1977). *Decision making: A psychological analysis of conflict, choice, and commitment.* New York: Free Press.

Krumboltz, J. D., Mitchell, A. M., & Jones, B. G. (1978). A social learning theory of career selection. In J. M. Whitely & A. Resinkoff (Eds.), *Career counseling* (pp. 100–127). Monterey, CA: Brooks/Cole.

Lanning, W. (1982). The privileged few: Special counseling needs of athletes. *Journal of Sport Psychology, 4,* 19–23.

Lederman, D. (1988, December 7). Players spend more time on sports than on studies, an NCAA survey of major college athletes finds. *Chronicle of Higher Education,* pp. A33–A38.

Petitpas, A., & Champagne, D. E. (1988). Developmental programming for inter-collegiate athletics. *Journal of College Student Development, 29,* 454–460.

Schafer, W. (1971). *Sport socialization and the school.* Paper presented at the Third International Symposium on the Sociology of Sport, Waterloo.

Schultz, R. W. (1960). Problem solving behavior and transfer. *Harvard Educational Review, 30,* 61–77.

Selby, R., Weinstein, H. M., & Bird, T. S. (1990). The health of university athletes: Attitudes, behaviors, and stressors. *Journal of American College Health, 39,* 11–18.

Skinner, B. F. (1974). *About behaviorism.* New York: Knopf.

Smallman, E., Sowa, C. J., & Young, B. D. (1991). Ethnic and gender differences in student athletes' responses to stressful life events. *Journal of College Student Development, 32,* 230.

Spreitzer, E., & Snyder, E. E. (1989). Sports involvement and quality of life dimensions. *Journal of Sport Behavior, 12,* 3–11.

Vacc, N. A., & Loesch, L. C. (1987). *Counseling as a profession.* Muncie, IN: Accelerated Development.

CHAPTER 9

Athletics and Career Development: A Research Model

VICTORIA D. COLEMAN AND SHIRL A. BARKER

Student athletes are receiving greater attention as issues and concerns related to their personal, academic, and career development become more prominent. Our society is challenging educational institutions at all levels to become more accountable to the academic and career development interests of athletes. This chapter highlights STRATEGIES: A Model of Career Development for Student-Athletes (Coleman & Barker, 1991a), which was designed to meet the career concerns of this special population. The model consists of six components: (a) introduction and orientation; (b) self-assessment; (c) decision making; (d) educational, occupational, and community information; (e) preparation for work, leisure, and retirement; and (f) research and evaluation. Implications for counseling and development professionals are also discussed.

THEORETICAL FRAMEWORK

Self-assessment, the foundation of STRATEGIES: A Model of Career Development for Student-Athletes (Coleman & Barker, 1991a), has its antecedents in the theoretical framework of Super's (1957) developmental self-concept theory of vocational behavior. Super suggests that individuals attempt to implement their self-concept by choosing to enter the occupation they perceive as providing the most opportunity for self-expression. He also indicates that the specific behaviors individuals engage in are a function of their stage of life development. The model of career development for student athletes emphasizes self-assessment, self-concept development, and self-

81

esteem, which incorporate the identification of one's values, interests, abilities, and personality. The authors believe these four areas comprise the core of knowledge necessary for career exploration.

Self-Concept Development

Super, Starishevsky, Matlin, and Jordaan (1963) examined self-concept theory as it pertains to vocational development. They described self-concept development as consisting of the processes of *formation*, *translation*, and *implementation* of self-concepts.

Formation. The process of formation begins during infancy when the child begins to develop an identity as a person, and continues, typically, through preadolescence. Formation consists of five activities: (a) exploration; (b) self-differentiation; (c) identification; (d) role playing; and (e) reality testing. Through exploration, the individual investigates self and environment and distinguishes one from the other. Self-differentiation occurs when the individual can say "This is me; that is someone or something else." Identification is the individual's attempt to be like someone else, such as a parent, sibling, or significant other. Role playing involves "trying on" various roles to see how they fit, and includes evaluation of the persons identified with those roles. Reality testing takes place when the individual applies the emerging self-concept in real-life situations such as childhood play, extracurricular activities, and part-time employment (Super et al., 1963).

Translation. Translation of self-concepts into vocational terms may occur through one or more of three activities: identification with an adult may lead one to play that person's occupational role; experience in a role in which one is cast, by choice or by accident, may facilitate the discovery of attributes which have vocational relevance; and observation may lead to the identification of personal attributes which are applicable in a particular kind of work (Super et al., 1963).

Implementation. The implementation or actualization of self-concepts occurs as one is beginning professional training or as one completes formal education and enters an occupation (Super et al., 1963).

Self-Esteem

Self-esteem, or self-acceptance, is a dimension of self-concept (Super et al., 1963). Specifically, self-esteem provides the feeling tone for the self-concept. People with high levels of self-esteem feel a sense of value and worth, like themselves, have confidence in themselves, and act accordingly. Those with low levels of self-esteem are doubtful about their own worth, see themselves as undesirable, often feel anxious, depressed, and unhappy, and have little faith or confidence in themselves. Thus, feelings of high or low self-esteem can profoundly affect the way a person plans for, enters, adjusts to, progresses in, and leaves occupational endeavors or other life experiences (Super et al., 1963).

Student athletes with high self-esteem will feel good about themselves and perform at a high level academically and athletically. Those with low self-esteem may not have positive attitudes about themselves, and consequently will probably have more difficulty achieving success in the classroom and in their respective sports.

It is within the constructs of self-esteem and vocational development that STRATEGIES: A Model of Career Development (Coleman & Barker, 1991a) was conceptualized.

REVIEW OF THE LITERATURE

There is an expanding body of literature on the personal and career development of student athletes, and interest in this topic continues to increase. Chartrand and Lent (1987) discussed the growing concern of academic administrators and student affairs professionals for the academic and personal development of student athletes. Sparent (1988) indicated the need for developing an understanding of the links between the students' academic world and their athletic world. Maud and Fletcher (1986) pointed out that academic counselors are assuming greater responsibility in the career development of athletes.

Phelps (1982), criticizing procedures that result in the student athlete entering the work world with no marketable skills, recommends extensive vocational counseling. Research by Kennedy and Dimick (1987) suggests that student athletes have lower career maturity than other students. According to Petitpas and Champagne (1988), the lower career maturity levels may be attributable to the fact that sports provides the student athlete with a strong enough identity that he or she may not engage in the exploratory behavior that is necessary for career and personal development. As long ago as 1976, McFarland found that student athletes showed significant academic improvement after a career counseling program. Nelson (1982) had similar results.

Unfortunately, there is not much literature on programs that help athletes with their academic and career concerns. However, a guide was developed by Schwartz (1988) to help athletes relate their skills to the world of work, and Petitpas and Schwartz (1990) have designed a model to help athletes identify their transferable skills.

Gurney, Robinson, and Fygetakis (1983) conducted a survey of NCAA Division I schools and found that the academic support services for student athletes, when they existed, were often using untrained staff and inadequate programs.

While the literature reflects a growing awareness of the uniqueness of career programs for student athletes, much remains to be developed and researched. With the recent reforms and changes in policy established by the NCAA, and possible future legislation, more comprehensive programs for student athletes are imperative.

STRATEGIES: A MODEL OF CAREER DEVELOPMENT

STRATEGIES: A Model of Career Development for Student-Athletes (Coleman & Barker, 1991a) includes six components: (a) introduction and orientation; (b) self-assessment; (c) decision making; (d) educational, occupational, and community information; (e) preparation for work, leisure, and retirement; and (f) research and evaluation.

Introduction and Orientation

The purpose of this component is to introduce the concept and process of career development and to provide a working definition. Career development is defined as an ongoing, lifelong process, beginning at birth and continuing throughout life. It focuses on the acquisition of information and skills about self and the world of work. As a concept, career development differs from the traditional idea of career education and vocational guidance in that the goal of career development is to facilitate the self-actualization of the individual, rather than to simply respond to labor market demands. Career development is an important aspect of personal, academic, and athletic endeavors.

Self-Assessment

In this component, which is the foundation of the career development process, the individual carefully examines four personal variables—values, interests, abilities, and personality—as they relate to career development. Values are significant in that when one chooses a career, one is choosing a value system and a life-style. Exploration of both vocational and avocational interests helps the person identify potentially enjoyable career activities. Abilities, achievements, and accomplishments, along with personality type, also help determine what might be appropriate career endeavors for a given individual.

Assessment and evaluation of intelligence, learning styles, academic deficiencies, and cultural influences are undertaken in connection with the examination of the aforementioned personal factors (Coleman & Barker, 1991b). From the academic and personal information, an individual learning plan is designed and correlated with athletic performance and career concerns.

All of the above information should assist an individual in responding appropriately to the question "Who Am I?" Coleman (1989) believes that self-assessment is the most critical element in the career development process.

Decision Making

Decision making is also a critical component. Principles, strategies, and styles of decision making are explored, with particular emphasis placed on identifying the student athlete's strategies and styles. The authors do not contend that any one strategy or style is better than another. Rather, any given strategy or style might afford the opportunity to make positive, satisfying, and appropriate decisions. For example, individuals may utilize one strategy for career decisions, another strategy for decisions related to the family, and yet a third strategy for decisions involved with their athletic performance.

Educational, Occupational, and Community Information

By gathering educational, occupational, and community information, students can identify the occupational and professional opportunities for the 1990s and the 21st century, and learn about the educational requirements for those opportunities. Resources such as educational institutions, business and industry, fraternal and athletic organizations, alumni, and community agencies are highlighted for their contribution to the career development process.

Preparation for Work, Leisure, and Retirement

This component focuses on the basic elements of the job search, such as resumé preparation, interviewing, and job maintenance skills. Students are encouraged to consider how their leisure and recreational time can be used to advance self-actualization. Specifically, student athletes must understand that their athletic skills and talents are transferable to other career opportunities. With the average life span increasing, and with retirement assuming a different role in our society, career development should also include preparation for the later life stages.

Research and Evaluation

Research and evaluation are essential components of STRATEGIES. The authors' own research has utilized pretest-posttest methodology to measure the self-esteem, vocational maturity, and decision-making skills of student athletes. The Tennessee Self-Concept Scale (Roid & Fitts, 1988) is used to measure self-esteem, the Attitude Scale of the Career Maturity Inventory (Crites, 1978) measures vocational maturity, and the Problem Solving Inventory (Heppner, 1988) measures the student athlete's ability to make appropriate decisions. The authors believe that this research design is appropriate for the model of career development. A closer examination of the following barriers may also be considered.

BARRIERS TO THE CAREER DEVELOPMENT OF STUDENT ATHLETES

In the process of career development, student athletes often encounter barriers such as low self-esteem, inadequate decision-making skills, and lack of information. Coleman (1989) and Coleman and Barker (1991c) have identified several barriers that are experienced by members of multicultural and diverse populations, and have categorized them as internal or external. Internal barriers are related to the self, while external barriers tend to focus on the environment. Some internal and external barriers that can impede student athletes' career development are:

Internal Barriers
low self-esteem
lack of confidence
conflict between personal values and athletic goals
fear of failure and/or success
level of career maturity
inadequate decision-making skills
lack of marketable skills
lack of previous work experience
lack of general information
life-stage conflicts relating to role of athlete
public image issues

External Barriers
few role models
lack of mentors
stereotypes
racism and discrimination
admission criteria
family expectations
societal expectations
socioeconomic status
inadequate educational preparation
lack of career and vocational guidance
ethnic background of counselor
athlete-coach perceptions
inadequately trained support staff
conceptualization of work ethic
peer pressure to adopt a particular norm
adapting to the college/university environment

It is important for counselors and other professionals who work with student athletes to determine to what extent these barriers are adversely affecting the career development of this population. By making appropriate interventions, professionals will be better able to facilitate the career development of student athletes. Interventions might include individual and group counseling that focuses on values clarification and how to make better decisions, workshops that address the identification and utilization of transferable skills, and specific instruction relating to public image (e.g., etiquette, appropriate dress, and communicating with the media). Cross-cultural communication training for individuals working with student athletes can also facilitate the success of academic and career development programs.

MYTHS AND REALITIES

There are a number of myths related to the career development of student athletes, and these frequently interfere with the career development process.

Myth: Athletic scholarships are an important way to achieve a successful career.

Reality: Athletes participating in revenue-producing sports, especially minority students, graduate at a very low rate. An NCAA study of entering Division I athletes indicates that 42.5% of Black athletes left college in bad standing, compared to 19.6% of White athletes leaving college (Lederman, 1991). In the view of Richard Lapchick, director of the Northeastern University Center for the Study of Sport in Society, these statistics suggest that a disproportionate number of Black athletes were kept on a nongraduating track, so that by the time their eligibility expired they were so far from graduating that they may have dropped out due to lack of hope (Lederman, 1991). The overall graduation rate of student athletes at Division I schools has been reported to be 56.1% ("Graduation Rates," 1991).

Myth: Proposition 48 is restoring academic integrity to college athletics and providing career security for student athletes.

Reality: NCAA Propositions 48, 28, and 42 restrict educational access, especially for Black athletes, and are less than effective in reducing the exploitation of student athletes by colleges and universities (Cheatham and Associates, 1991). (See chapter 11 for further discussion.)

Myth: Student athletes who do not go on to a professional career in sports have few job skills.

Reality: Most student athletes possess a number of unique skills which, if marketed effectively, can lead to future career success. These transferable skills can be used in any field the athlete chooses to enter (Bolles, 1991; Petitpas & Schwartz, 1990).

Myth: Participation in athletics gives student athletes the confidence and exposure needed to make positive career choices.

Reality: Student athletes face a variety of difficulties in regard to career development. These difficulties include lack of identification of academic and career plans, unrealistic goal setting, and lack of self-confidence outside of the athletic arena (Remer, Tongate, & Watson, 1978; Sowa & Gressard, 1983).

Myth: At least for the few student athletes who ultimately make it into the professional arena, the career education programs currently in place will prove adequate.

Reality: Few professional athletes play beyond their 40s (Lerch, 1981). For some team sports such as baseball, basketball, and football, the average athletic longevity is about 5 to 7 years (Andreano, 1973; Biltz, 1973). Career education must prepare even future professional athletes for a time when they will have to choose a new occupation.

Myth: Academic support and career development services are equally available to minority and White athletes.

Reality: Present academic support and career education systems have been designed to remedy the problems encountered by White, middle-class students. Black and White students show vast differences in academic preparation before college (Lederman, 1991). Differences in learning styles and communication styles are also noted for minority students (Jacobs, 1987). Most academic support personnel, from mentors and tutors to upper-level administrators, are untrained in the skills required to deal effectively with student athletes from varied cultural backgrounds.

Myth: Talented athletes can bypass a college education as a step in their career development. If they are not academically prepared for college studies, athletes can go directly into professional programs.

Reality: Colleges are well recognized as the route to using athletic talent to make financial gains in professional careers, especially in football and basketball (Atwell, 1989).

Myth: Most student athletes accepted by 4-year colleges and universities are qualified to do the academic work required for success in a career, if they apply themselves.

Reality: Twenty percent to 30% of high-school-graduate football and basketball players are functionally illiterate (Atwell, 1989).

The aforementioned myths and realities illustrate the need for career development programs that are designed to assist student athletes at all educational levels.

IMPLICATIONS AND RECOMMENDATIONS

There are significant implications for personal, academic, and career counselors, as well as other professionals, who provide services for student athletes or who want to promote the success of these individuals. The various implications apply to the areas of research, counseling, training, program development, and policy.

Research

Opportunities for research are abundant, and there is considerable need for research related to the student athlete. While literature does exist, there is a dearth of research related to the concerns of student athletes and their success in elementary school, secondary school, postsecondary education, and beyond. New paradigms and models must be created in order to facilitate and incorporate a better understanding of student athletes. Developmental problems, the effects of academic and psychological support services, and cross-cultural training are but a few of the topics requiring further investigation.

Counseling

It is apparent that student athletes require personal, academic, and career counseling in order to facilitate their success at all educational levels and later in the work force. Elementary schools, high schools, colleges, and universities must take the initiative and responsibility for establishing and implementing programs that provide the necessary support systems for this special population. Traditional counseling techniques may not be appropriate for different races, ethnic groups, and cultures. Additionally, professional counselors must assess their own cultural identities to determine how they might influence the career counseling process.

Training

The authors strongly recommend that individuals who plan to provide services for student athletes receive specialized training in order to work with this group. Since student athletes have different issues, needs, and concerns, traditional training in counseling and related areas may not be sufficient. Of particular interest is training in multicultural relations and cross-cultural communication, as an increasing number of athletes come from multicultural and diverse backgrounds. Counselor educators should consider expanding the curricula to include the study of special populations, specifically student athletes.

Program Development

The literature indicates that programs related to the issues, needs, and concerns of student athletes can have a positive impact on their personal, academic, and career development. However, there is still a tremendous deficiency of such programs. Therefore, counseling and development professionals need to critically examine their role in designing personal, academic, and career counseling programs for student athletes.

Policy

As the NCAA and educational institutions at all levels become more involved in establishing legislation, policy, and guidelines for student athletes, professionals who work with this population must take active roles as advocates for this special group. Counseling and development personnel possess the knowledge, skills, and talents to influence policy that will affect the student athlete.

As the public demands accountability from educational institutions, academics and athletics are facing new challenges for the 1990s and for the 21st century. Consequently, there has been an increasing institutional response to the special needs of student athletes, and a growing belief that solely addressing academics is not the solution. Holistic approaches and comprehensive models allow the student athlete to build on those skills that have contributed to present successes while addressing those areas that are problematic. Accordingly, it is now acknowledged that the improvement of personal, academic, and career services for student athletes is an institutional responsibility.

CONCLUSION

It is apparent that the success of student athletes is contingent upon a variety of support services. Consequently, career development and related programs are a critical component of student achievement. Educational institutions must be committed to the design, implementation, research, and evaluation of career development models to ensure success of such programs. New paradigms are evolving as institutions acknowledge their responsibility for facilitating the academic success of student athletes. STRATEGIES is an attempt to promote this success.

References

Andreano, R. (1973). The affluent baseball player. In J. T. Talamini & C. H. Page (Eds.), *Sport and society* (pp. 308–314). Boston: Little Brown.

Atwell, R. H. (1989, May 18). [Testimony to subcommittee on postsecondary education.] Washington, DC: U.S. House of Representatives, Committee on Education and Labor.

Biltz, H. (1973, Summer). The drive to win: Careers in professional sports. *Occupational Outlook Quarterly, 17*(2), 2–16.

Bolles, R. N. (1991). *What color is your parachute?* Berkeley: Ten Speed Press.

Chartrand, J. M., & Lent, R. W. (1987). Sports counseling: Enhancing the development of the student-athlete. *Journal of Counseling and Development, 66*, 164–167.

Cheatham, H. E., & Associates. (1991). *Cultural pluralism on campus.* Alexandria, VA: American College Personnel Association.

Coleman, V. D. (1989). *A model of career development for a multicultural workforce.* Unpublished manuscript.

Coleman, V. D., & Barker, S. A. (1991a, Spring). A model of career development for student-athletes. *Academic Athletic Journal*, pp. 33–40.

Coleman, V. D., & Barker, S. A. (1991b, Fall). Academic counseling for student-athletes: A model. *Academic Athletic Journal*, pp. 13–19.

Coleman, V. D., & Barker, S. A. (1991c). Barriers to the career development of multicultural populations. *Educational and Vocational Guidance*, *52*, 25–29.

Crites, J. M. (1978). *The career maturity inventory*. Monterey, CA: CTB/McGraw Hill.

Graduation rates of athletes and other students at Division I colleges: A *Chronicle* survey. (1991, March 27). *Chronicle of Higher Education*, p. A39.

Gurney, G. S., Robinson, D. C., & Fygetakis, L. M. (1983, Spring). Athletic academic counseling with NCAA Division I institutions: A national profile of staffing, training, and service. *Athletic Administration*, pp. 9–12.

Heppner, P. P. (1988). *Problem-solving inventory*. Palo Alto, CA: Consulting Psychologists Press.

Jacobs, R. L. (1987). *An investigation of the learning style differences among Afro-Americans and Euro-American high, average, and low achievers*. Unpublished doctoral dissertation, Peabody University, Louisiana.

Kennedy, S. R., & Dimick, K. M. (1987). Career maturity and professional sports expectations of college football and basketball players. *Journal of College Student Personnel*, *28*(4), 293–297.

Lederman, D. (1991, July 10). Black athletes who entered college in the mid-80's had much weaker records than Whites, study finds. *Chronicle of Higher Education*, pp. A30–A32.

Lerch, S. H. (1981). The adjustment to retirement of professional baseball players. In S. L. Greendorfer & A. Yiannakes (Eds.), *Sociology of sport: Perspectives* (pp. 138–148). New York: Leisure Press.

Maud, B., & Fletcher, H. J. (1986). The N4A: Ten years old and changing. *Academic Athletic Journal*, *3*, 1–14.

McFarland, D. (1976). Career planning and academic success for the student athlete. *Athletic Administration*, *11*, 16–17.

Nelson, E. S. (1982). The effects of career counseling on freshman college athletes. *Journal of Sport Psychology*, *4*, 32–40.

Petitpas, A., & Champagne, D. E. (1988). Developmental programming for intercollegiate athletes. *Journal of College Student Development*, *29*(5), 454–460.

Petitpas, A., & Schwartz, J. (1990, June). *Assisting student-athletes in understanding and identifying transferable skills*. Paper presented at Counseling Student-Athletes Conference, Springfield, MA.

Phelps, M. (1982). The student-athlete: A proposal. *College Board Review*, *124*, 14.

Remer, R., Tongate, F. A., & Watson, J. (1978). Athletes: Counseling the overprivileged minority. *The Personnel and Guidance Journal*, *56*, 626–629.

Roid, G. H., & Fitts, W. H. (1988). *Tennessee Self-Concept Scale: Revised manual*. Los Angeles: Western Psychological Services.

Schwartz, M. (1988). *The athlete's guide to understanding and identifying transferable skills*. Springfield, MA: Springfield College.

Sowa, C., & Gressard, C. (1983). Athletic participation: Its relationship to student development. *Journal of College Student Personnel*, *24*, 236–239.

Sparent, M. E. (1988, April). *The student-athlete in the classroom: Developmental issues affecting college athletes and their impact on academic motivation and performance*. Paper presented at the Annual Symposium on Developmental/Remedial Education, Albany, NY.

Super, D. E. (1957). *The psychology of careers*. New York: Harper and Row.

Super, D. E., Starishevsky, R., Matlin, N., & Jordaan, J. P. (1963). *Career development: Self-concept theory*. New York: College Entrance Examination Board.

CHAPTER 10

The Negative Stereotyping of Student Athletes

KEVIN L. BURKE

All clients are affected to some extent by the stereotypes associated with the groups to which they belong or the life roles they play. Student athletes face a unique set of stereotypes which can affect the way they see themselves and the way they interact with others. Some prejudgments made on the basis of the student's role as athlete might be positive ones. For instance, athletes are generally considered to be driven, dedicated, and hardworking, at least on the court or the field. But there are also several negative stereotypes with which student athletes must contend. The counselor who is aware of these stereotypes and who can understand their possible effects on the individual will be better able to serve the student-athlete client. The first stereotype addressed here, the notion that most athletes are not intelligent, affects both male and female student athletes. The other stereotypes to be discussed are specific to female student athletes.

THE "DUMB JOCK" IMAGE

Because mind and body have historically been viewed as separate and because there is a tendency to assume that one or the other is dominant in any given individual, many people cannot imagine that a person could excel both athletically and academically. Thus, athletes are often presumed to be unintelligent. Some research appears to offer factual support for this commonly held belief. A study by Purdy, Eitzen, and Hufnagel (1985) found that student athletes tend to have lower grade point averages than other students. The same study revealed that student athletes are admitted to college under special circumstances more often than are nonathletes, and that students admitted under special circumstances generally deliver a poor academic performance. An American Institutes for Research (1988) study found that student athletes had lower grade point averages than did students involved in other types of extracurricular activities.

However, care must be taken in the interpretation of such findings. Many student athletes are reinforced for their athletic skills starting at an early age and are not encouraged to balance their athlete role with a strong effort in the classroom. The effect of the self-fulfilling prophesy can never be ruled out. Furthermore, other researchers have reached different conclusions about the "dumb jock" stereotype's basis in reality. A number of studies (Braddock, 1981; Curry & Jiobu, 1984; Henschen & Fry, 1984; Wulf, 1985) indicate that student athletes perform as well as or better than their nonathlete peers and graduate at the same or a higher rate.

The myth that athletes lack the intelligence or self-discipline to succeed academically is perpetuated by the media's focus on those student athletes who do poorly in the classroom or who engage in delinquent or illegal behavior. Rarely do the newspapers or television newscasts highlight those athletes who are also accomplished students. In addition, many nonathlete students resent the privileges and social status that athletes enjoy. Out of jealousy or insecurity, these students sometimes help to sustain the belief that their athletic classmates are intellectually inferior (Figler & Whitaker, 1991).

The dumb jock image is attributed to both male and female student athletes, but is more strongly associated with males. Several studies (Birrell, 1987; Kiger & Lorentzen, 1986; "NCAA Study," 1991) have found that female college athletes do perform better academically than their male counterparts. The stereotype is also more heavily associated with players of team sports than with participants in individual sports like tennis, golf, and gymnastics. Purdy, Eitzen, and Hufnagel (1985) found that students competing in individual sports had higher graduation rates than football, basketball, and baseball players. Again, such research results must be considered with a critical eye.

Being labeled as a poor student can have a direct impact on the student athlete. For instance, the student may experience dissonance in terms of self-esteem; the role of athlete might enhance feelings of self-worth while at the same time the role of student is bringing about feelings of inferiority. In response, the student may retreat from academic endeavors, needing to believe that education is not as important as athletics. Like any individual who is perceived by others as having only one area of achievement, the student athlete who is valued only for his or her athletic abilities will suffer emotionally.

For the professional counselor working with the student athlete, the objective is to help that individual develop as a multidimensional human being. The counselor can assist the student athlete by exploring ways to balance the dual roles of athlete and student. For those who have difficulty coping with the time demands of both their sport and their classes, time management skills can be a significant step toward improving academic performance. If an athlete lacks confidence or self-esteem in terms of academics, the counselor can assist in exploring the basis for that low self-esteem and can encourage the athlete to incorporate the student role as an important part of his or her identity.

On a larger scale, the myth of the academically inferior athlete can be countered from two angles. First, to the extent that student athletes really do have difficulty in academics, changes in policy and services are in order. Many such changes are already underway. The NCAA has endorsed some proposals to more closely monitor the academic progress of student athletes (Wieberg, 1991). New entrance and academic requirements are intended to put every student athlete in a position to graduate after no more than 5 years. In addition, academic counseling services are already in place in many institutions. By raising the emphasis on academics and by insisting that athletes put forth their best effort in the classroom, administrators, faculty members, and counselors can help restore the balance between sports and academia.

Second, inasmuch as the stereotype arises from misconceptions, it should be addressed from a public image standpoint. The many student athletes who do keep athletics and academics in proper perspective are currently virtually invisible. More publicity surrounding the academic achievements of student athletes would go a long way toward dispelling the notion that most athletes are poor students. Generally, the media tends to focus on academic problems and rule infractions. But with some effort on the part of college and university public relations officers, the academic success stories can gain increased attention as well.

STEREOTYPES OF FEMALE STUDENT ATHLETES

Early sports were developed by men for men (Curry & Jiobu, 1984). The ancient Greeks, operating under the belief that women's involvement in sports would destroy their femininity, excluded women from the Olympic games (Coakley, 1990). Echoes of such early attitudes persist in today's society, affecting the socialization process of young girls and sustaining the stereotypes associated with women who participate in sports.

One prevalent myth is that women are too delicate or too susceptible to injury to participate in sports (Coakley, 1990; Curry & Jiobu, 1984; Figler & Whitaker, 1991). Many misinformed people also are still of the opinion that athletic participation will damage reproductive organs or cause childbearing complications. In actuality, injury rates for women are no greater than those for men (Wells, 1985), and women who are in good physical condition generally have easier childbearing (Coakley, 1990).

Because sports has traditionally been a male domain, women who are associated with athletics now must contend with the widely held belief that women's involvement with sports causes a "masculinization" process of some kind. That is, many people seem to believe that the competition, exertion, and physical conditioning of athletics will diminish a woman's "feminine" qualities and foster in her qualities which are considered more appropriate to men. In particular, there is a concern that female athletes will become aggressive and competitive, traits traditionally considered "unbecoming" in a woman, and that they will develop large muscles and begin to look more like men. A related myth is that female athletes, especially the more successful ones, are usually physically unattractive (Coakley, 1990).

Of course, societal attitudes about femininity and masculinity are changing, and today's female athlete is often seen as androgynous rather than as masculine or feminine (Burke, 1986; Figler & Whitaker, 1991; Harris, 1985). In general the well-conditioned body is considered attractive in both men and women (Coakley, 1990). However, many aspects of gender-specific socialization persist, often leading to role conflict or role confusion in the female athlete.

Related to the idea that sports participation causes masculinization in women is the stereotyping of women athletes as lesbians (Figler & Whitaker, 1991). Members of the general public tend to associate "masculine" traits in women with homosexuality in women. (The belief that all lesbians look and act like men is, of course, just another myth.) Therefore many women are suspected of being lesbian simply by virtue of their participation in sports. According to Bennett et al. (1989), homophobia is rampant in women's sports. Likewise, Figler and Whitaker (1991) state that "a hostile cloud of homophobic suspicion hovers over all of female sport. It disheartens female athletes, hinders female coaches, and is a likely factor in the reluctance of the media to promote professional sport for women" (p. 330).

The "cloud of homophobic suspicion" can affect the female athlete in a variety of ways, depending on her actual sexual orientation, her comfort with it, and her overall psychosocial development. Those female athletes who are indeed leading a lesbian life-style but are not open about their sexuality may fear exposure. Those who wish to be "out of the closet" may feel oppressed by coaches or teammates who, wishing not to have the sport or team associated with lesbianism, encourage them to keep this aspect of their identity a secret.

Because the level of acceptance of homosexual behavior is still low in this culture, heterosexual women involved in athletics may fear the stigma and mistreatment attached to lesbianism. As a result, they might feel threatened by their lesbian counterparts on the team, or feel compelled to make clear statements, through their behavior, dress, and words, about their own "normal" sexual identity and femaleness. For instance, some female athletes use "role signs" such as nail polish, jewelry, makeup, and hair ribbons to enhance the feminine look (Curry & Jiobu, 1984).

Curry and Jiobu (1984) discuss some other ways in which female athletes might respond to the stereotypes about women in sports. They point out that some female athletes, recognizing that athletic endeavor is just as appropriate for women as it is for men, simply disregard the gender issues and participate in sports with no concern about the judgments of the larger society. Other female athletes engage in what is known as *role splitting*; that is, they take on "masculine" traits during competition but exude "femininity" in most other aspects of their lives (Curry & Jiobu, 1984).

Of course, not all female athletes exhibit physical and psychosocial traits traditionally considered "male," and not all female athletes are lesbians. Female athletes are a diverse group, and as women's participation in sports increases and becomes more visible, society is gradually becoming aware of this diversity. Furthermore, negative attitudes toward both androgyny and lesbianism are beginning to soften as members of society become educated about the realities of both gender roles and homosexuality.

Cultural attitudes are slow to change, though, and therefore counselors working with female student athletes need to be aware of the effects of stereotypes on this population. Female student athletes are likely to bring with them to counseling issues of gender-role confusion and sexual orientation whether they are "feminine," "masculine," or androgynous and whether they are heterosexual, lesbian, or bisexual. In order for the female student athlete to be effectively served, these issues will often need to be addressed directly.

CONCLUSION

As administrators of athletic programs in the schools and colleges become more sincerely concerned with the academic development of the students, and as sports become recognized as the domain of both men and women, the stereotypes associated with all student athletes may weaken and finally disappear. Until that time, these stereotypes and myths must be acknowledged and addressed appropriately through counseling and education. As counselors and other professionals utilize their knowledge of the effects of such stereotypes and work to educate those who perpetuate them, the dual role of student athlete will become more enjoyable and satisfying for both young men and young women.

References

American Institutes for Research. (1988). *Summary results from the 1987–88 national study of intercollegiate athletes* (Report No. 1). Palo Alto, CA: Center for the Study of Athletics.

Bennett, R. S., Duffy, A., Kalliam, D., Martin, M., Smith, N. J. W., West, E. L., & Whitaker, K. G. (1989). Homophobia and heterosexism in sport and physical education: Why must we act now? *CAHPERD Journal Times, 51*(8), 16–18.

Birrell, S. (1987–88). The woman athlete's college experience: Knowns and un-knowns. *Journal of Sport and Social Issues, 11*(1–2), 82–96.

Braddock, J. (1981). Race, athletics and educational attainment: Dispelling the myths. *Youth and Society, 12*, 335–350.

Burke, K. L. (1986). Comparison of psychological androgyny within a sample of female college athletes who participate in sports traditionally appropriate and traditionally inappropriate for competition by females. *Perceptual and Motor Skills, 63*, 779–782.

Coakley, J. J. (1990). *Sport in society: Issues and controversies* (4th ed.). St. Louis: Times Mirror/Mosby.

Curry, T. J., & Jiobu, R. M. (1984). *Sports: A social perspective*. Englewood Cliffs, NJ: Prentice-Hall.

Figler, S. K., & Whitaker, G. (1991). *Sport and play in American life* (2nd ed.). Dubuque, IA: William C. Brown.

Harris, D. V. (1985). Personality in sport participants. In L. K. Bunker, R. J. Rotella, & A. S. Reilly (Eds.), *Sport psychology: Psychological considerations in maximizing sport performance* (pp. 24–29). Ithaca, NY: Mouvement Publications.

Henschen, K. P., & Fry, D. (1984). An archival study of the relationship of inter-collegiate participation and graduation. *Sociology of Sport Journal, 1*(1), 52–56.

Kiger, G., & Lorentzen, D. (1986). The relative effects of gender, race and sport on university academic performance. *Sociology of Sport Journal, 3*(2), 160–167.

NCAA study: More Whites graduating. (1991, June 23). *Pantagraph Newspaper*, p. 7.

Purdy, D., Eitzen, D. S., & Hufnagel, R. (1985). Are athletes also students? The educational attainment of college athletes. In D. Chu, J. O. Segrave, & B. J. Becker (Eds.), *Sport and higher education* (pp. 221–234). Champaign, IL: Human Kinetics.

Wells, C. L. (1985). *Women, sport & performance: A physiological perspective*. Champaign, IL: Human Kinetics.

Wieberg, S. (1991, June 27). Colleges take control, address academics, coaches' income deals. *USA Today Newspaper*, p. 7C.

Wulf, S. (1985, January 7). The diploma bowl. *Sports Illustrated*, p. 7.

CHAPTER 11

The African American Student Athlete

WYATT D. KIRK AND SARAH V. KIRK

The African American population is considered to be overrepresented in organized sports. African American athletes have thus been the subject of much controversy and research in recent years. Counselors who work with athletes in higher education settings can better serve this population if they become aware of the issues and conditions that affect its members. This chapter will explore the historical involvement of African Americans in sports, debunk some of the current myths, discuss the specific problems that minority athletes face, and provide guidelines for counseling the African American student athlete.

HISTORY OF AFRICAN AMERICANS IN SPORTS

African Americans have always been participants in this country's sporting events, from the days of legalized slavery to the present. History informs us that as a group of people African Americans have always respected physical activity and sports. Athletic participation was a standard part of every African child's upbringing. Anthropological evidence and eyewitness accounts indicate that several sports were routinely enjoyed in the African villages (Ashe, 1988).

These athletic activities were not just for fun. They also met several sociological needs, including the following:

1. *General fitness skills.* The mimicking of certain animals in gymnastics and exercises such as running, swimming, climbing, and wrestling, taught speed, endurance, flexibility, and strength.

2. *Economic survival skills.* Stick fighting, running, swimming, row-
   ing, fishing, and hunting were skills necessary to the maintenance of villages.
3. *Civics and cooperative values.* The teamwork involved in sports
   such as tug-of-war instilled a sense of solidarity and cooperation
   in village inhabitants.
4. *Military skills.* In the event of organized conflict, skills in stick
   fighting, riding, and archery were necessary for survival.

These athletic skills were brought from Africa to the newly colonized
America, but as slaves the first African Americans were not always permitted
to exercise them (Ashe, 1988). Restrictions against athletic activity affected
slaves and indentured servants alike and were often based on the religious
beliefs of their European owners and employers (Baker, 1981). However,
despite restrictive laws such as the "Black Codes," African American slaves
and "free Negroes" found opportunities to engage in and enjoy sports such
as running, fishing, and town ball (a form of baseball). African Americans
were the nation's best jockeys and boxers even before the Civil War and
the Emancipation Proclamation. Later, during the 19th century, the YMCA
provided African Americans with facilities and opportunities to train athletically and to become the first of a wave of trained sports administrators. In
1953, with the establishment of the first "colored" YWCA, African American
women were provided an opportunity for athletic training. Then came sports
at the college level, which were encouraged and supported by the private
Black colleges. Administrators at these colleges had to be careful, though,
not to offend their benefactors, who might have viewed such activities as
frivolous and nonacademic.

It was expected that when the second Merrill Act was passed in 1890
these new Black land-grant institutions would be able to legitimately fund
recreational facilities. However, White southern congressmen arranged for
the federal funds authorized by the Act to be channeled through state legislators. For many years, the money went primarily to the White institutions,
leaving the predominantly Black colleges without adequate support (Ashe,
1988). Still African Americans persevered in attempting to legalize their role
in sports.

Currently the skills of African American athletes are recognized and
utilized at both the collegiate and the professional levels. In fact, in the late
1940s, when African Americans began regularly participating in athletics at
predominantly White colleges and universities, their enrollment sparked an
interest on the part of the fans which led White universities to compete with
Black colleges for potentially valuable athletes.

But the African American student athlete has not always fared well on
these campuses. Through the years many have spoken out against racism and
embarrassment. As early as 1917, Paul Robeson, a Rutgers University All-

American and later a well-known actor, voiced his protest of the unfair treatment of Black athletes. In 1968, the Olympic games in Mexico were boycotted in an attempt to break the "system of athletic slavery" (Edwards, 1969).

There were also early protests by African American student athletes, including those at the University of California at Berkeley, the University of Texas at El Paso, the University of Kansas, and Michigan State University, just to mention a few. Among the controversial issues were the disallowance of an "Afro" hairstyle, the absence of African American girls on the pom-pom team, and the lack of African American coaches (Green, Smith, Gunnings, & McMillan, 1974). In 1972, African American protests came to a peak at Michigan State University. After several African American student athletes, faculty members, administrators, and researchers had observed and analyzed discriminatory athletic practices, a group of concerned professors presented a detailed protest to the leaders of the Big Ten Conference. This protest was based on a report, "The Status of Blacks in the Big Ten Athletic Conference: Issues and Concerns," which "showed that fairness and equal opportunity were a myth in collegiate sports and that the patterns of racial discrimination found in society were also found in U.S. athletics" (Green et al., 1974, p. 11). There were three areas that were of prime concern: (a) the problems experienced by African American athletes as a function of their race, (b) the number who fail to graduate, and (c) the lack of African American representation at all levels of employment, especially as coaches and officials (Greene et al., 1974).

Twenty years later these same three areas are still of grave concern. A recent NCAA survey of the graduation rates of African American athletes indicated that of those who entered college in the 1984–85 academic year only 26.6% graduated, compared to 52.2% of Whites (Johnson, 1991).

The data also suggest that the treatment of African American athletes, both students and professionals, has not changed significantly. However, some athletes and nonathletes do indicate that things have improved and that teammates and fans express less overt racism than they did in the past (Johnson, 1991). Conversely, many respondents to a USA Today poll felt that certain positions, such as quarterback and pitcher, demand thinking and leadership skills that are usually not considered attributes of African Americans. Both Black and White respondents to the poll ranked leadership as the highest attribute of White athletes, followed by thinking, instincts, strength, and speed. Both groups also listed the skills of the African American athlete in the exact reverse order (Myers, 1991). Clearly, if this poll is any indication, racist attitudes are not a thing of the past. Most African Americans interviewed did agree that some form of prejudice and discrimination still exists in sports, though it is perhaps less blatant than in the past. Evidence of discrimination is further substantiated by the fact that African Americans are still underrepresented in the areas of management and coaching—again at both the college and professional levels.

MYTHS AND REALITIES

Let us now turn our attention to some persistent myths that continue to plague African American athletes. African American student athletes should be made aware of as many of these myths as possible, and should be informed about the attending realities. Otherwise they will be at risk for buying into the myths and subsequently making poor choices.

Myth: Sports Is a Vehicle for Social Mobility

One dangerous myth is the belief that Black athletes enhance their social mobility through sports. The sports literature has given considerable attention to the phenomenon of upward mobility, particularly as it relates to the African American athlete. Dubois (1974) suggests that for African American athletes sports is a significant vehicle by which to become socially mobile.

However, not all studies support the contention that social mobility is enhanced through sports. Rather, two opposing views emerge in the literature—the traditional view and the contemporary view (Dubois, 1974). The traditional view adopts the premise that sports enhances mobility and therefore considers sports as a vehicle for Black mobility. In the contemporary view, on the other hand, sports is seen as a reflection of the society's development and not necessarily as a means to social mobility. In more recent literature, Rudman (1986) indicates that whether athletic success is regarded as a vehicle for social mobility may be a function of social orientation and what he terms the "culture of poverty." In other words, according to Rudman, the less affluent in our society, irrespective of race, are likely to see sports as a means of social mobility.

Sailes (1990), in a position paper presented at the Annual National Conference of the North American Society for the Sociology of Sport, addressed the myth and reality of upward mobility as follows:

> If the African American male is successful in sport, particularly if he
> becomes a sports star, the rewards are social prestige, recognition,
> and status. College scholarship offers usually find the most talented,
> gifted African-American athletes. Unfortunately, over 75% of Black
> athletes playing NCAA Division I basketball and football never gradu-
> ate and fewer than 1% ever sign a professional sports contract. (p. 6)

Lide (1981) found, when he interviewed African American football players who were attempting to adjust to retirement, that many were left bitter and disappointed at the lack of success and social mobility. More than half of those interviewed expressed that their major problem was financial, and only about half had plans for a second career. From the above-mentioned data and research, it is obvious that the notion of sports as a stepping stone to high status is, for the most part, a myth where the African American athlete is concerned (see chapter 13).

Myth: Black Athletes Are "the Brawn"

Another myth characterizes Black athletes as "the brawn" in the brawn-versus-brain dichotomy. Brains are generally associated with the abilities of White athletes to lead and to think, while brawn is associated with the ability of African American athletes to eclipse their White counterparts physically. In addition, African American athletes who achieve fame in sports are often perceived as having succeeded almost with no effort or intensive training. While John Elway and Jim Kelley are applauded by fans and the media for their hard work, Doug Williams and Warren Moon are described as naturally gifted athletes. The basic assumption beneath these kinds of statements is that Black athletes run faster and are more naturally physical, while White athletes are leaders and thinkers.

Sports provides some of the nation's most familiar images in Black and White, images that reinforce the prejudicial view that Whites should be quarterbacks, coaches, and managers and Blacks should be running backs, sprinters, and basketball stars (Myers, 1991). Historically, researchers and theorists have taken various positions to explain the supposed differences between the abilities of Black and White athletes. First, there is the biological explanation, which suggests that African American athletes' skeletal and muscular development gives them an innate physiological advantage in some types of athletic competition. For example, LeFlore (1982) contends that the musculature and physiognomy of Black men make them more naturally adapt and proficient in sports like boxing, baseball, basketball, track, and football than in other sports, such as swimming.

Another explanation is based on the belief that fundamental differences exist between Black and White athletes. Williams and Youssef (1975) found that college football coaches described Black players in terms of physical speed, quickness, and high achievement motivation. Whites, on the other hand, were rated high on reliability and quick thinking skills. But such findings reflect stereotypical views rather than actual differences. White and African American athletes alike are confronted with these kinds of stereotypes daily. Though some scientific studies do point to subtle physical differences (Sailes, 1984), it has not been demonstrated that those differences significantly affect athletic performance (Cobb, 1936; Jordan, 1969; Malina, 1975; Metheny, 1939; Petty & Steggerda, 1940). For example, research shows that success by any group is dependent upon cultural differences and socialization, in any avenue of human performance, and is largely determined by certain constructs, such as opportunity, availability of resources, and the level of individual dedication to success.

Myth: Sports Has Helped to Decrease Racism

Because the life-styles and triumphs of highly successful Black athletes are regularly highlighted in the media, there is now a widespread misconception that sports has helped reverse racial prejudice and discrimination. In reality, sports has not eliminated racism. Rather, the sports world, a microcosm of the wider society, in many cases serves to mask some of the more serious truths. Despite wishful thinking to the contrary, athletics is no different from any other social institution. Beyond the glamour and excitement, we still find overt and subtle acts of racism.

Many authors have addressed the myth that sports has decreased racism. For example, Chu (1982) states as follows:

> Sports, it is presumed, has "done something" for Blacks. Much of this thinking has unfortunately been anecdotal, journalized and unsystematic. Sport sociology literature contains empirical evidence of the existence of institutionalized discriminatory practice (in the areas of recruitment policy, position assignment, performance expectation, reward, authority structure and salary) in collegiate and professional circles. Some of these racist practices are more or less directly demonstrable; others are more subtle, requiring inferential leaps. (p. 162)

Lapchick and Slaughter (1989) note that African American athletes have continuously expressed concern over the racism they have encountered in the areas of treatment, recruitment promises, academic advisement, discipline, position allocation, and segregation. Additionally, there is concern about exploitation. Racism at the intercollegiate level is well documented (Edwards, 1972; Green et al., 1974; Lapchick & Slaughter, 1989; Loy & McElvoyce, 1970). While there has been some improvement in racial attitudes, for the most part racism, prejudice, segregation, and discrimination remain intact in both intercollegiate and professional sports.

Obviously, other myths continue to persist, but the three discussed above are considered by researchers and athletes alike to be the most constant and pervasive. If counselors and other professionals are to work effectively with African American student athletes, they must remain mindful of these myths and of the attending realities.

CONCERNS OF AFRICAN AMERICAN COLLEGIATE ATHLETES

Along with an understanding of the myths and stereotypes associated with African Americans in athletics, professionals should bring to their work with these students an appreciation of the issues most often faced by Black student athletes. Being African American and a college student and an athlete means dealing with a variety of fears and concerns unique to that constellation of roles. The more prominent of those concerns center on academic preparation, loneliness and isolation, time management, and faculty expectations.

Academic Preparation

Like other athletes, African American athletes come to college to become educated, but often their educational background has not prepared them for the rigors of academia. Unfortunately, many of them have received the message that there is no need to make any effort in the classroom. With the focus almost entirely on athletic achievement, they may end up "majoring in eligibility" (Leach & Conners, 1984). While many colleges and universities have begun to create academic support services for their athletes, the problem remains (Edwards, 1991). Too often academic advisors and counselors lack a comprehensive understanding of underprepared African American student athletes and their academic and career goals.

Therefore, when appropriate the academic advisor/counselor must take into account both the real and the assumed educational limitations of these young people and assist them in reaching the academic performance level expected of a college student. Through exploring the student's academic history, study habits, abilities, and attitudes, the counselor can better understand the nature of the problem and the probable solutions. On a day-to-day basis, the counselor can help the student develop the skills necessary for successful completion of regular assignments. With help, many underprepared students can eventually "catch up" to their classmates.

Loneliness and Isolation

African American student athletes at predominantly White colleges and universities often have a difficult time making the transition from high school to college. Many experience loneliness and isolation because coaches and athletic personnel keep them away from the nonathletic student body at an important time in their adjustment. Ruffer made the following comment in 1971:

> The black athlete may experience severe loneliness and isolation, be harassed by white team members to make him feel intellectually inferior and socially unacceptable, be resented by the white athletic establishment when he develops friendly relationships with white girls, and be subjected to name calling and derogatory remarks by coaches and players. (p. 12)

Almost 20 years later, these behaviors still persist, and African American student athletes continue to deal with these and many other pressures as they attempt to balance academics, athletics, and personal relationships. There is a central need, then, to clarify the fact that these athletes are important members of the collegiate establishment and to ensure that their adjustment in all areas will be normal. The counselor must insist that these young people are provided with opportunities to interact with their nonathlete peers and to attend to all aspects of their personal development.

Time Management

Like most student athletes, African American student athletes are subject to the time pressures of practice, training, and travel. They may become frustrated in their attempts to find adequate time for both study and sports. It is particularly difficult for them to coordinate their busy schedules in a way that will allow them to take advantage of the academic resources and services available on campus (Jordan & Denson, 1990). Preventative programming is needed to assist these students with time management skills. If the goal of attending college is to obtain a degree as well as to participate in athletics, then academic advisors and counseling services must be integral components in the university's response to the unique needs of the African American student athlete.

Faculty Expectation

While African American student athletes are glorified for their athletic prowess on the one hand, they are often considered suspect in terms of academic ability on the other hand. Many faculty members still believe that African American student athletes cannot master college-level courses. As a result, these students often receive very little intellectual support and attention. Professors may "let them off easy," assuming they cannot do the work. Leach and Conners (1984) noted that Black student athletes walk a thin line between admiration and resentment. They are often viewed as both hero and scoundrel (Green et al., 1974). The arrogance in the university community toward African American student athletes is well documented, and adds to the adjustment difficulties they often encounter. One testimony that best illustrates how faculty members may feel toward student athletes is the example of one academic advisor talking with a prospective student athlete who wanted to attend the university in question. The advisor told the young person, "If you don't have good study habits, if you don't want to do the work, and if you can't do the work, don't come here. It's not easy to be a student athlete here. Professors don't know you, and if they do know you, they probably won't like you."

What then do we as concerned human service professionals do to support our African American student athletes? One option, of course, is counseling. Let us briefly explore the potential positive impact of counseling on this group.

COUNSELING THE AFRICAN AMERICAN STUDENT ATHLETE

> Colleges and universities are supposed to be, along with parents and religious organizations, the guardians of our nation's moral values. When discrimination is part of the hiring system, when exploitation is part of the recruiting process, when athletes do not get an education, our nation's institutions of higher education have forfeited that guardianship. (Lapchick & Slaughter, 1989, p. 55)

The need for effectiveness in counseling student athletes has been espoused for nearly two decades (Chartrand & Lent, 1987; Goldberg, 1991;

Hawthorne, 1971; McFarland, 1976; Remer, Tongate, & Watson, 1978; Wittmer, Bostic, Phillips, & Waters, 1981). Also over the past 20 years, literature has revealed that administrators and faculty at predominantly White colleges tend to disregard the special needs of African American students (Green et al., 1974; Leach & Conners, 1984).

Edwards (1991) makes the following point about White academic advisors and counselors on predominantly White campuses:

> The resulting ineptitude was greatly compounded when the target of counseling efforts were African American student athletes because, among far too many of these advising personnel, ignorance of the overall African American experience in education was rivaled only by a lack of understanding regarding the institutions dynamics and character of big-time collegiate sport and the evolving roles of African Americans in it [sic]. (p. 28)

Edwards (1991) also notes that statistical data shows that 65% to 75% of African American athletes who matriculate on White campuses on athletic scholarship never receive a diploma. What then are some of the problems that counselors must address in working with the African American student athlete?

First and foremost, not only must counseling (both academic and personal) be made available to these athletes, but they must be encouraged—and required, when necessary—to avail themselves of the counseling services. Second, the counselors, along with possessing the appropriate skills, must be willing to view these young people as just that—young people who are attempting to attain a college degree. Counseling practice with African American student athletes must take into account the history, values, and beliefs of the African American culture as well as the sociopsychological characteristics of the individual student. The counselor must accept that the experience of African American student athletes is unique. Their personality development is strongly influenced by the psychocultural dynamics of today's society, which often cause them feelings of uncomfortableness. Therefore, in working with the African American student athlete, the counselor must also concentrate on self-esteem building as it relates to the real world, not just the world of sports. With aware and knowledgeable counselors, social workers, and other human service personnel to assist them, surely more African American students will be able to successfully complete college.

Aside from understanding the social, cultural, and developmental factors that affect African American student athletes, counselors should also be aware that certain techniques and theoretical approaches tend to be more effective with this population. For instance, according to Vontress (1971), particular attention should be paid to counselor attitude, structuring, language transference, countertransference, self-disclosure, personalism, attending behavior, and resistance. Other techniques of equal importance include group counseling, information giving, consultation, follow-up, referral, reassurance, modeling, confrontation, role playing, and homework assignments. In terms of theoretical approach, African American student athletes generally respond most favorably to existentialism, gestalt, client-centered counseling, reality counseling, rational emotive therapy, and behaviorism.

CONCLUSION

There are many other issues of paramount importance surrounding the plight of the African American student athlete. While we have not enumerated all of them in this chapter, others will be explored in other chapters throughout the book. We hope that the salient issues discussed here will raise the level of sensitivity of our readers. Unfortunately, there is still a need to strengthen all support services to athletes in general and African American student athletes specifically if education is to remain the centerpiece of the student athlete's involvement.

References

Ashe, A. (1988). *A hard road to glory: A history of the African-American athlete—1919–1945*. New York: Warner Books.

Baker, W. J. (1981). *Sports in modern America*. St. Louis: River City.

Chartrand, J. M., & Lent, R. W. (1987). Sports counseling: Enhancing the development of the athlete. *Journal of Counseling and Development, 66*, 164–167.

Chu, D. (1982). *Dimensions of sports studies*. New York: John Wiley and Sons.

Cobb, M. W. (1936). Race and runners. *Journal of Health and Physical Education, 7*, 3–9.

Dubois, P. E. (1974). Sports, mobility and the Black athlete. *Sociology Bulletin, 3*, 40–61.

Edwards, H. (1969). *The revolt of the Black athlete*. New York: Free Press.

Edwards, H. (1972). The myth of the racially superior athlete. *Intellectual Digest, 44*, 32–38.

Edwards, H. (1991). Democratic pluralism: Placing African American student athletes in the context of a new agenda for higher education. *National Academic Advising Association Journal, 11*, 28–122.

Goldberg, A. D. (1991). Counseling the high school student athlete. *The School Counselor, 38*, 332–333.

Green, K. L., Smith, G. S., Gunnings, T. S., & McMillan, J. H. (1974). Black athlete educational, economic and political considerations. *Journal of Non-White Concerns in Personnel and Guidance, 3*, 6–27.

Hawthorne, J. J. (1971). Responsibilities for the academic success of student athletes. In E. S. Steiz (Ed.), *Administration of athletes in colleges and universities* (Vol. 1). Washington, DC: American Association for Health, Physical Education, and Recreation.

Johnson, W. O. (1991, August 5). The Black athlete. *Sports Illustrated*, pp. 39–41.

Jordan, J. (1969). Physiological and anthropometrical comparisons of Negroes and Whites. *Journal of Health, Physical Education, and Recreation*, pp. 93–99.

Jordan, J. N., & Denson, E. L. (1990). Student services for athletes: A model for enhancing the student athlete experience. *Journal of Counseling & Development, 69*, 95–97.

Lapchick, K. E., & Slaughter, J. B. (1989). *The rules of the game: Ethics in college sports.* New York: Macmillan.

Leach, B., & Conners, B. (1984). Pygmalion on the gridiron: The Black student athlete in a White university. In A. Shriberg & F. R. Brodzinski (Eds.), *Rethinking service for college athletes* (pp. 31–49). San Francisco: Jossey-Bass.

LeFlore, J. (1982). Athleticism among American Blacks. In R. M. Pankin (Ed.), *Social approaches to sports* (pp. 104–121). East Brunswick, NJ: Associated University Press.

Lide, W. E. (1981). *Forced retirement among former professional football players with short-termed careers.* Unpublished doctoral dissertation, Ohio State University.

Loy, J. W., & McElvoyce, J. F. (1970). Racial segregation in American sports. *International Review of Sports Sociology, 5,* 5–24.

Malina, R. (1975). Body weight, stature, and sitting height in White and Negro youths 12–17 years. *United States Vital and Health Statistics Survey, Series 11,* Number 26.

McFarland, D. (1976, Fall). Career planning and academic success for the student athlete. *Athletic Administration, 11,* 16–17.

Metheny, E. (1939). Some differences in bodily proportions between American Negro and White male college students as related to athletic performance. *Research Quarterly, 10,* 41–53.

Myers, J. (1991, December 16). What's the difference? Studies inconclusive. *USA Today,* p. 4C.

Petty, C., & Steggerda, M. (1940). An anthropometric study of Negro and White college women. *Research Quarterly, 11,* 110–118.

Remer, R., Tongate, R. A., & Watson, J. (1978). Athletes: Counseling the overprivileged minority. *The Personnel and Guidance Journal, 56,* 616–629.

Rudman, W. J. (1986). The sport mystique in Black culture. *Sociology Journal, 3,* 305–314.

Ruffer, W. A. (1971). Symposium on problems of the Black athlete. *Journal of Health, Physical Education and Recreation, 2,* 12.

Sailes, G. (1984). *Sport socialization comparisons among Black and White adult male athletes and nonathletes.* Unpublished doctoral dissertation, University of Minnesota.

Sailes, G. (1990). *Facts and figures on the Black athlete.* Bloomington: Indiana University.

Vontress, C. E. (1971). Racial difference: Impediments to rapport. *Journal of Counseling Psychology, 18,* 7–13.

Williams, R. L., & Youssef, Z. I. (1975). Division of labor in college football along racial lines. *International Journal of Sport Psychology, 6,* 3–13.

Wittmer, J., Bostic, D., Phillips, T. D., & Waters, W. (1981). The personal, academic and career problems of college student athletes: Some possible answers. *The Personnel and Guidance Journal, 60,* 52–55.

PART III

EXTERNAL FORCES AND THE ATHLETE

CHAPTER 12

The Media's Effect on Athletics

CHARLES S. FARRELL

Intercollegiate athletics needs the media. Media coverage helps sell tickets and attract "blue chip" athletes. Conversely, the media need athletes to help sell their product. This chapter offers the perspective of one sports journalist regarding the impact the media and sports have upon each other, and chronicles the parallel growth of these two major American institutions.

During the 1980s three of journalism's most coveted awards and a Pulitzer Prize have gone to newspapers for their investigative stories on college sports. Such acknowledgment clearly underscores the media's increasing devotion to sports, a devotion that has a drastic effect on the course of athletics and points to the ever-expanding effect of the media on athletics.

Sports has always received solid coverage by the media, which realized that sports offered a safe and consistent divergence from the somber news pages. Almost every person can let his or her mind drift and place himself or herself in the role of a sports hero, scoring the winning touchdown or breaking the tape first in the 100-meter dash. Not everyone is an active participant in sports; many experience sports vicariously through the media.

The first sports newspaper in this country, the *America Turf Register*, which covered horse racing, was founded in 1829. The second, *Spirit of the Times*, started in 1831. Others soon followed. Within a few years, the New York newspapers began covering sports on a regular basis, escalating the acceptance of sports as a serious form of journalism. The expansion of baseball westward and its increasing popularity were largely the result of the newspaper coverage of that era. In the 1870s, Joseph Pulitzer took the dynamic step of separating sporting news from the rest of the newspaper in his *New York World*. Within a few years, all major newspapers had followed Pulitzer's lead.

Newspapers were the primary source of sports information in the early years of this country's history. Although newspapers and magazines continue to have a great impact on sports coverage, it was the advent of the electronic media that sent sports into a new stratosphere.

College sports had begun emerging as exciting, entertaining spectator events from the onset of the first college football game on November 6, 1869. That same year, Guglielmo Marconi discovered that sound could be transmitted without wires or cables, giving birth to the radio. In 1899, the Associated Press hired Marconi to transmit the first news over radio; the subject was international yacht races.

Over the next 20 years, radio was further developed as an entertainment and journalistic medium. Other technological inventions like the telephone, the telegraph, and the typewriter also helped expand sports coverage, but radio had the most profound impact. Within a few years, radio stations were linked together to form national networks, on which sports were a main event. The 1921 heavyweight championship fight between Jack Dempsey and Georges Charpentier received major radio attention; the 1927 Rose Bowl game was the first radio program to be broadcast coast-to-coast.

As television evolved, it quickly became the medium of opportunity for sports. Thousands of people who never had the chance to attend a sporting event were entertained in the comfort of their own homes.

With the emergence of television came major advertising dollars; college and professional sports organizations flocked to the networks for the money and exposure. As televised sports grew, so did the money involved. Along with the money came increasing pressures to succeed. Illegal college recruiting and payments to players were rampant by the late 1940s. In 1948 the NCAA established a compliance committee to enforce its rules and regulations. Within a year, the compliance committee had gained enough evidence to charge seven institutions with offering scholarships to athletes without regard for their financial need. The committee also estimated that as many as 20 other institutions had violated the rules.

Scandals in college sports, and the media's revelations of such scandals, expanded during the 1950s and 1960s. In 1951, the New York District Attorney discovered that more than 30 basketball players at seven colleges had engaged in point shaving—winning or losing basketball games by less than the betting point spread. There were also revelations of illegal recruitment of players. The scandal severely reduced the stature of New York collegiate basketball and dramatically underscored the potential for unethical behavior in college athletics.

At about the same time, the success of one legendary team shriveled when three of the team's players were convicted of participating in gambling and point shaving. For the first time, the NCAA put a school on probation and canceled basketball for a year.

But college sports continued to soar, enhanced by the exposure and money that television offered. Newspapers and magazines, in an effort to keep pace, increased the amount of time and space devoted to sports. General stories were shortened or eliminated to provide the space for additional coverage of more and more sports events as their popularity grew. Not only were college sports getting more attention, but the so-called "minor" sports, such as running, golf, and sailing, also received coverage as they captured the interest of the populace.

The 1960s, 1970s, and 1980s brought the period of greatest ascendancy for college sports. As the revenue became higher and higher, colleges jockeyed for advantages by continuing to resort to illegal methods of securing players to lead them to championships. Hunter K. Rawlings III, president of the University of Iowa, discussed at one of the NCAA conferences the control that television exerts over collegiate athletics, which has led to recruiting scandals and abandonment of academic responsibility.

All too frequently, the recruiting scandals and academic laxity involve Black athletes. As segregation ended and the Civil Rights Movement swelled, many colleges began to open their doors to Blacks, and the benefits of having Black athletes soon became evident. But many of these Black athletes tended to be less prepared for college than their White counterparts. And, because they also tended to be less economically well off than Whites, Black athletes were more susceptible to the lure of monetary rewards for their athletic ability. Unfortunately, there always seemed to be someone who was prepared to change high school transcripts or someone who was willing to let them slide academically. Many of these Black athletes found themselves out on the streets once their eligibility expired, uneducated and unprepared for life.

The athletic exploits of Black athletes, both college and professional, were well documented by the media, but their exploitation tended to be ignored, with one notable exception. In the July 1, 1968 issue of *Sports Illustrated*, sportswriter Jack Olsen sought to explode the myth of sports by discussing the intolerance that Black athletes have experienced despite appearances of acceptance, and the dissatisfaction and disillusionment of Black collegiate and professional athletes. Olsen's articles were an exception in their time, as most of the media chose to concentrate on what happened on the playing field, rarely straying from that safety.

Much of the media's caution sprang from its cozy relationship with the sports establishment. The media needed sports, knowing that its coverage of athletics meant increased sales of newspapers and magazines as well as advertisements. Many sportswriters and broadcasters also enjoyed the perks of free admission to sporting events, free meals while covering them, and "friendships" with players, which meant they had a lot to lose if they suddenly turned traitor and exposed the seamier sides of athletics.

That mindset may have its greatest impact on the public's perceptions of Black athletes, as the media continues to present stereotypical images. A few brave sports journalists have abandoned the cautious attitude, however. For instance, in 1987 Derrick Jackson presented in *New York Newsday* a stinging commentary on the realities of Blacks in athletics. Jackson described the system that stereotypes Blacks as having inborn athletic talent and Whites as being smart—the thinkers.

Thus, the age of media innocence on important issues began to fade as a few bold members of the media began to apply to athletics the same journalistic standards found in reporting about government, education, and international affairs. Perhaps they were forced into this more serious approach by the escalation of scandals in college sports. After all, two thirds of the top 100 competitive NCAA institutions served some sort of sanction during the 1980s. The situation reached such proportions that 80% of college presidents interviewed in an NCAA survey a few years ago said they believed intercollegiate athletics interfered with the educational mission of their institutions, and 70% of the American public related that they felt that intercollegiate athletics was out of control.

Since the media responds to and reflects public demand, several investigations into scandals in college sports ensued. Some of the more notable ones exposed the payment-to-athletes scandal at a southern university, improprieties at another institution, and academic fraud at a southeastern university. Interestingly, most of the stories were pursued by journalists other than sports reporters. The aura of hypocrisy shines brightly as journalists direct light on problems to which the media's own publicity machines contributed.

Mary Kress, the assistant managing editor for special coverage at the *Florida Times-Union*, explained the use of nonsports journalists to expose the scandals at a conference on Media Economics and Sports Coverage in the fall of 1987:

> In sports, we'd rather have an investigative reporter come in and do
> our tough reporting so that the sports beat reporter doesn't get in
> trouble with the coach or the players. The beat reporter gets a tip
> that could lead to a very good news story, but he doesn't pursue it.
> He passes it on the investigative reporter and he does it. The beat
> reporter goes back and covers the game and hobnobs with the players
> and hangs out in the locker room.
>   . . . Part of the problem may be that . . . readers want to know
> what happened at the game. And there's a lot of truth to that: The
> readers don't necessarily want to know all of the hard news stories
> that are there for the doing. But I don't think the readers really care
> about Chile or Tibet either, and we certainly don't have any lack of
> conscience in telling them about those things in our national and in-
> ternational news sections.

Kress's suggestion at a recent conference that readers do not want to know the hard news behind their favorite teams gains credibility from what happened after the *Lexington Herald-Leader* published its account of improprieties in the basketball program at one state university. More than 400 readers canceled their subscriptions within hours after the article was published; bomb threats were directed at the paper, and journalists were subjected to verbal abuse and physical threats.

While fans may react with vehemence to attacks on their teams, the increasing scrutiny by the media has had a massive effect on college sports. The media is often criticized for its tendency to confirm the separation of sports from the main university mission. The exposés generally focus on the negative aspects of college sports—the illegal recruiting, academic fraud, payments to players—rather than on positive stories about the educational, social, and cultural opportunities intercollegiate sports can provide. But those negative aspects, and their exposure in the media, have forced intercollegiate athletics down a path of reform aimed at bringing intercollegiate athletics within the mission of education.

Proposition 48 was perhaps the first monumental step toward reform in intercollegiate athletics, and it received, and continues to receive, massive media coverage as its effects continue to be felt. Media scrutiny of the measure mushroomed over complaints that the regulation was biased against Blacks, who tend not to do as well on standardized tests as their White counterparts. The controversy, if it did nothing else, pointed to continuing racial dilemmas that permeated not just college sports, but higher education in general. For the first time, race, a dominant social issue, was being regularly addressed on the sports pages.

And the media continues its scrutiny as intercollegiate athletics struggles to provide quality education and at the same time field entertaining, winning teams. At the 1991 NCAA convention, a pivotal agenda of reform was adopted overwhelmingly, embraced even by those who have purely athletic interests. The reform movement is expected to continue for a number of years.

The media will undoubtedly continue its scrutiny, pressed on by the prospects of more Pulitzers or perhaps by a renewed attention to the unwritten ethical code that good journalists are supposed to follow. But the media must undergo some reforms of its own if it is to increase its effectiveness in the area of sports reporting. First, there must be a reconciliation of the hypocrisy involved in acting as both publicity agent and voice of conscience for sports. Wilford Bailey, former president of the NCAA, advocates assigning more investigative reporters to sports departments (Bailey & Littleton, 1991). Bailey and Littleton (1991) have also called for an end to the gambling interests and for increased coverage of women and minorities in sports.

CONCLUSION

Sports journalism has come a long way from its origins, and it has had a profound effect on athletics. Most of the information about sports and sports stars comes from the media, and the media is, to a great extent, responsible for making sports such a dominant influence, particularly in the Black community. But the widespread influence of sports journalism brings with it the responsibility to consistently separate myth from reality. Through responsible reporting aimed at raising the public's level of awareness (Bailey & Littleton, 1991), the media can become a strong and positive force in determining the future direction of collegiate athletics.

References

Bailey, W. S., & Littleton, T. D. (1991). *Athletics and academe: An anatomy of abuses and a prescription for reform.* New York: Macmillan.

Kress, M. (1987, September 1). Speech presented at Conference on Media Economics and Sports Coverage, Columbia University, New York.

Olsen, J. (1968, July 1). The Black athlete: A shameful story. *Sports Illustrated,* p. 6, 12–27.

Additional Resources

Ashe, A. (1988). *A hard road to glory: A history of the African-American athlete— 1919–1945.* New York: Warner Books.

Dealy, F. X., Jr. (1990). *Win at any cost: The sell-out of college athletics.* Secaucus, NJ: Carol Publishing Group.

Lapchick, R. E., & Slaughter, J. B. (1989). *The rules of the game: Ethics in college sports.* New York: Macmillan.

Lawrence, P. R. (1982). *Unsportsmanlike conduct: The National Collegiate Athlete Association and the business of college football.* New York: Praeger.

Moyes, N. B., & White, D. N. (1974). *Journalism in the mass media.* Needham Heights, MA: Ginn and Company.

Stephens, M. (1988). *A history of news: From the drum to the satellite.* New York: Viking Penquin, Inc.

CHAPTER 13

The Role of the NCAA

WILFORD S. BAILEY

> Intercollegiate athletics programs shall be maintained as a vital component of the educational program and student-athletes shall be an integral part of the student body. The admission, academic standing and academic progress of student-athletes shall be consistent with the policies and standards adopted by the institution for the student body in general. (National Collegiate Athletic Association [NCAA], 1991b)

This "principle of sound academic standards," one of 13 principles for the conduct of intercollegiate athletics set forth in its Constitution, expresses concisely the primary role of the NCAA in achieving the proper relationship between academics and athletics for college student athletes. Since this principle addresses implicitly their academic preparation for admission to and satisfactory progress in college, it also has tremendous implications for the student athlete in high school and even in lower grades.

Attention must be focused immediately on a myth that continues to have tragic consequences for many young students, especially minorities—the belief that sport is their principal avenue to fame and fortune. That this is indeed myth, rather than reality, is documented vividly by Gates (1991), who reports the following figures: In the U.S., where there are 1,200 African American professional athletes, there are 12 times more African American lawyers, 2½ times more African American dentists, and 15 times more African American doctors. At each level of sports participation from high school through the pros, competition becomes tighter and the odds of making the team become slimmer (see Table 1). Thus, educational preparation for other fields of endeavor is essential. In its role as regulator of intercollegiate athletics, the NCAA has taken on the challenge of ensuring that college

Table 1. Estimates of High School Participants in Football and Men's Basketball Who Achieve College and Professional Status

Status	Football	Basketball
Number high school senior participants	265,000	150,000
Number making teams of NCAA institutions (freshman)	16,450	3,800
Number playing seniors	8,930	2,400
Number making cut, professional teams	215	64

Note. From *Athletics and Academe: An Anatomy of Abuses and a Prescription for Reform* (p. 84) by W. S. Bailey and T. L. Littleton, 1991, New York: Macmillan. Copyright 1991 by American Council on Education and Macmillan Publishing Company. Reprinted by permission.

athletes receive educations that will prepare them for productive lives once their sports careers are over.

A brief history of intercollegiate sports reveals the difficulties the NCAA has faced in its efforts to achieve that goal expressed in the above principle. For nearly 50 years after the first American intercollegiate contest in 1852 (crew, between Harvard and Yale), college sports were operated by students as a part of their extracurriculum. By the turn of the century, most colleges and universities in our nation had established faculty boards of control, and intercollegiate athletics were being transferred into the institutional structure for governance. This change was the result of concerns about a number of improprieties in college sports, not the least of which had to do with the academic status of participants.

As Smith (1988) documents, the question of eligibility was causing particular concern in the 1890s, due in large part to the fact that individuals were transferring with impunity from one college to another merely to participate in athletics. In an extreme manifestation of this type of abuse, one midwestern university football team had several members who had no connection at all with the university (Smith, 1988).

After the NCAA was organized in 1906, the Association's efforts were directed primarily to establishing game rules and to working with game officials. In 1922, a 10-point code was adopted in which member institutions were urged to, among other things, adopt eligibility rules. Even though the eligibility rules for NCAA championships began to get more specific in the late 1940s, it was not until 1965 that the NCAA membership adopted a meaningful eligibility requirement—the "1.600 rule," requiring incoming student athletes to have a predicted grade point average (GPA) of 1.600 (based on a maximum of 4.000) in order to be eligible for athletics grant-in-aid and to participate in an institution's program (Falla, 1981).

This eligibility requirement was applied for only a few years, for reasons which Falla (1981) summarizes well: concerns about interference with institutional autonomy and responsibility; questions about the validity of predictive tests; changes in the social structure of the nation, particularly the marked increase in federally funded college-aid programs for disadvantaged students; and an increase in the number of colleges adopting "open-door" admissions policies.

The NCAA membership abolished the 1.600 rule at its 1973 convention and, in its place, adopted the 2.000 rule (for Division I). The 2.000 rule required graduation from high school with a minimum GPA of 2.000 for all courses taken, for which there were no subject requirements. Many critics argued that the 2.000 rule was essentially meaningless as a measure of academic preparation for success in most colleges and universities, and the experience of the following decade proved them correct. Unfortunately, in far too many institutions student athletes were permitted, and indeed often helped, to circumvent, in one way or another, the academic requirements for students generally. The emphasis was on maintaining their eligibility. During that decade there was widespread exploitation of elite athletes by colleges and universities across the country. The institutions used outstanding athletes to generate winning records and consequently increase the visibility of their athletic programs, particularly those in football and basketball. Increased visibility, of course, meant increased revenue.

When the freshman eligibility requirement commonly referred to as Proposition 48 was adopted in 1983, to be implemented in 1986, more meaningful satisfactory progress requirements were adopted for immediate implementation. Having taken this action, the NCAA made plans to initiate a 10-year research project to evaluate the academic performance of student athletes at Division I institutions. The subjects were divided into five cohort groups, the first of which included student athletes on full or partial athletic scholarships who enrolled in the fall of 1984. This timing was designed to have two cohort groups enrolling before the implementation of Proposition 48 and three enrolling after it was in place, with all groups to be followed for 5 years.

The Proposition 48 eligibility requirement (a minimum GPA of 2.000 on 11 core courses and a minimum score of 700 on the SAT or 15 on the ACT[1]) has not been without controversy. The proposition has been challenged particularly with regard to the appropriateness of the fixed cut score on the precollege test and to its more negative impact on African Americans and other individuals of color. However, it is widely agreed that the requirement has had a positive influence in helping students achieve better preparation for satisfactory performance in college. While Proposition 48 and the satisfactory progress requirements have helped overcome some of the serious problems causing a fissure between athletics and the "other side of the house" of higher education, it is widely recognized that these academic requirements need to be strengthened if student athletes are to be adequately prepared to be successful in most colleges and universities as higher education moves to meet the challenges of the 21st century.

---

[1]On the revised ACT, the minimum score has been changed to 17, the score determined to have best concordance with 700 SAT.

Table 2. Proposed Modified Index for Core GPA and Precollege Test Score

GPA	SAT	ACT
2.500	700	17
2.375	750	18
2.250	800	19
2.125	850	20
2.000	900	21

[1]On the revised ACT, the minimum score has been changed to 17, the score determined to have best concordance with 700 SAT.

Therefore, the NCAA Presidents Commission is proposing changes in legislation to achieve the next step in strengthening academic requirements for Division I, with the new freshman eligibility requirements to be effective in 1995 and the changes in continuing eligibility requirements to be effective for student athletes enrolling in college in 1992. (Some of the changes are proposed for Division II also, but others are being deferred for consideration after more experience has been gained with current requirements.) The proposed changes for freshman eligibility include an increase in core courses from 11 to 13 (with the two additional courses to be in English and in either mathematics or the natural/physical sciences); an increase in minimum GPA on core courses from 2.000 to 2.500; and a modified indexing for the core GPA and precollege test score, retaining the minimum requirement of SAT 700 (or equivalent ACT) and 2.000 GPA on the core courses. Using the modified indexing, a student with a 900 SAT score and a 2.000 core GPA would be eligible (see Table 2).

Under the proposed changes, student athletes would be required to complete a progressive percentage of courses required for graduation in the specific degree program in order to maintain eligibility (25%, 50%, and 75% for eligibility in the third, fourth, and fifth years, respectively). In addition, the student's cumulative GPA would have to stand at 95% of the minimum GPA required for graduation in order for the student to be eligible in the third year, and at 100% of that minimum in order for the student to be eligible in the fourth and fifth years. (Note: The proposed legislation for satisfactory progress was amended to require 95% of the minimum graduation requirement for eligibility in the fourth or subsequent years.) The proposed changes would allow no more than 25% of the credit hours required for eligibility in a given academic year to be taken in the preceding summer, and would require certification of satisfactory progress for midyear transfers to be eligible at the beginning of the next academic year.

These proposed changes are supported both by conventional wisdom and by the findings of ongoing research by the NCAA on the academic performance of student athletes in Division I. It is widely recognized that additional core courses in English, mathematics, and the natural and physical sciences prepare students to be more successful in completion of their college degrees. NCAA research (NCAA Academic Requirements Committee, 1991) indicates that of student athletes who entered Division I institutions in 1984 or 1985—before Proposition 48 was implemented in 1986—those who met its requirements had approximately 10% higher graduation rates at the end of 5 years than those who did not. (For African American student athletes the difference was almost 20%.) Simulation analyses show that the proposed changes will further increase graduation rates.

Increasing the core GPA makes that standard more comparable to the test score in measuring academic preparation, and the modified indexing is widely recognized as a more equitable and educationally sound way of applying test scores and GPAs in evaluating academic preparation of students for college. Results of the current NCAA research show that "the equally weighted combination of core grade-point average and test score provides the single-best prediction of graduation" (National Collegiate Athletic Association, 1991a, p. 12).

Of particular significance is the fact that even though Proposition 48 has had a greater impact on African American student athletes than on others, the percent of African American student athletes on athletic scholarship in Division I was not appreciably lower in 1988 than in 1984—2 years after and 2 years before its implementation, respectively. The conclusion to be drawn from this is that most African American student athletes not meeting Proposition 48 requirements are being replaced by other African American students who do. Roberts (1989) predicted this outcome when he expressed the view that athletes who would receive scholarships under Proposition 48 would "be better and more motivated students who are far more likely to get a meaningful college education that will equip them to live successful and productive adult lives" (pp. 9–10) (see chapter 11).

Taken together, all the evidence leads to the conclusion that, with three years' notice, high school student athletes, with the encouragement of parents, counselors, and coaches, will better prepare themselves to be successful in their college work—and in life after college. In addition, it will be apparent to entering student athletes that they must make reasonable progress toward their degrees in order to continue their eligibility (see chapter 9).

Reference was made initially to the principle of sound academic standards and other principles for the conduct of intercollegiate athletics that are contained in the NCAA Constitution. Another of those is the "principle of competitive equity," which specifies that "the structure and programs of the Association and the activities of its members shall promote opportunity for equity in competition to assure that individual student-athletes and institutions will not be prevented unfairly from achieving the benefits inherent in participation in intercollegiate athletics" (NCAA, 1991b, p. 4). This principle obviously is one that must be taken into account in the setting of minimum academic requirements for student athletes in the several divisions and subdivisions of the Association's member institutions.

The Association's academic requirements for eligibility are minimum requirements, and conferences and individual institutions are expected to adopt and implement higher standards in keeping with their common interests and missions. In this context, it must be emphasized that the NCAA eligibility requirements for freshmen are *not* admission requirements. The latter are determined by the individual institution, as are requirements for continuation in residence for all students in the institution, which the student athlete is expected to meet. The minimum eligibility requirements adopted by the NCAA membership are to promote both competitive equity and the academic credibility of the member institutions. It is poor strategy for student athletes to "shoot for" the minimum requirement. Their sights should be much higher, and those who help influence them (parents, coaches, and counselors) should always encourage them to strive for higher goals academically.

Given the importance of sports in American culture, it is not surprising that some alumni may at times object strongly to academic requirements of "their institution" that they believe result in its student athletes being placed at a disadvantage to those of rival institutions. A striking example of this is seen in a recent formal request to the president of a major public university to reevaluate and change certain of its requirements in order to avoid placing its student athletes at an academic disadvantage. The alumni who submitted the request voiced concern about the university's developmental studies program for "at-risk" students, saying it keeps marginally prepared student athletes in the program for too long a time, and criticized the institution for its lack of a curriculum especially tailored to keep student athletes eligible.

Fortunately, the university president responded that he would "never compromise the academic integrity of the [university] in exchange for athletic victories" (Barnhart, 1991, p. D-8). It is pertinent to note that, in taking this position, he called attention to the national movement to strengthen academic standards. The same point was also made in an editorial in a major newspaper in the state commending the president for his strong stand on academic integrity: "The NCAA already is moving toward tougher educational standards. . . . The [university's] obligation is to turn out productive citizens. Vicarious alumni thrills come in a distant second" (Editor, 1991, p. A8).

Disgruntled alumni like those mentioned above reflect the values of a society in which sports has been given high status. The American culture itself strongly influences the evolution and current status of sports in our nation (Bailey & Littleton, 1991). In view of the relationship between sports and American culture, major changes affecting the relationship of sports and education can be made successfully only if some of the values attached to sports by society are modified. This point has been expressed well by Whalen (1991): "The reality is that we do have a sports-crazed society—one that is far more devoted to entertainment than to education. . . . [W]e have culturally cultivated an addiction for entertainment that has fed our tolerance for abuse" (p. 4).

While higher education must provide the leadership for changing the values attached to college sports in our society, and it is now doing this much more effectively than in recent decades, the problem is one that must be addressed at all levels of education. Strengthening the academic require- ments for freshman eligibility in the major colleges and universities accom- plishes little when high school student athletes and their coaches can successfully pressure a teacher to give a student athlete a higher grade than he or she earned based on the rationale that failure to do so would prevent the student from receiving an athletic scholarship and would thus preclude his or her opportunity to go to college.

The fact that some teachers are still willing to give student athletes grades they have not earned illustrates the pervasive and systemic nature of the imbalance between athletics and academics in our culture. One uni- versity president gave incisive expression to the problem when he stated:

> "I think that we just basically are saying that there's one thing in America important enough to set up separate rules for—the only thing important enough to society to really exempt you from many of the requirements of the university, and that's athletics. And don't think that our students don't see this. They accept it, don't challenge it, and carry that perception away with them into later life." (Bailey & Littleton, 1991, p. 32)

Helping our society, and helping individuals, understand the importance of the proper relationship between academics and athletics is of tremendous importance for the future of our nation as a competitor in a global economy and for the productive lives and welfare of individuals in our nation as we move into the 21st century.

Even for those student athletes who go on to play professional sports, an education is extremely important for a meaningful life. Tony Dorset, Heisman Trophy winner and 10-year veteran in the NFL, emphasized the importance of education in his message to blue chip recruits:

> If I had it to do over again I'd go back and apply myself a little more academically. I have friends who are pro athletes who can't even write a check, or they have to have their wives balance the check- book. That's sad. I know guys who've gone through the education sys- tem and still can't read. You better get a quality education while you can because when it is all over that's what you will have to depend on. (Ingram, 1990, p. F6)

It is obvious that the NCAA faces a tremendous challenge as it strives to create the proper relationship—a wholeness—between academics and athletics for college student athletes and to thereby promote this philosophy and practice for precollege education as well. Equally obvious is the fact that the Association has given too little emphasis to this responsibility throughout most of its existence. Fortunately, there are clear signs that this has changed and that the momentum for reform will continue. Under the leadership of the NCAA Presidents Commission and the Association's ex- ecutive director, Richard Schultz, and with the strong support of the NCAA

Council, priority is now being given to balancing academics and athletics and to the general issue of integrity in college sports.

In regard to NCAA legislation on the ethical conduct of students and coaches, young student athletes should be aware that the most frequent violations occur in the areas of recruiting and providing extra benefits to athletes. The principal problems in these areas are addressed in an NCAA guide for college-bound student athletes. High school coaches and counselors should ensure that every prospective college athlete is provided with a copy of the pamphlet, and they should also alert the student athlete that NCAA regulations are complex and can be broken unintentionally unless great care is exercised. Violation of these regulations can jeopardize the eligibility of a student to compete in intercollegiate athletics. Therefore, it is imperative that students know and comply with applicable rules.

CONCLUSION

As we await the outcome of the reform movement now underway, it must be emphasized that the NCAA is a voluntary organization of approximately 800 colleges and universities of great diversity. It is the membership, not some perceived hierarchy in Kansas City, that adopts and implements all its rules and regulations. As emphasized in the Knight Foundation Commission Report (1991), if the NCAA "did not exist, higher education would have to create it, or something very much like it. It is clear that a governing, rulemaking and disciplinary body of some sort is required" (p. 29). Therefore, success in achieving the proper relationship between academics and athletics will depend on the actions of the member institutions, both individually and collectively. It will be influenced also by the support, or lack thereof, received from alumni and friends of these institutions and from the public generally. Thus, it is obvious that society has a major role to play in achieving a proper relationship between academics and athletics at all levels of education in our nation.

If we are not successful in achieving that relationship in this decade, the only viable alternative may be amputation—eliminating intercollegiate athletics from the educational experience of our college students. That would be a great loss for all concerned.

References

Bailey, W. S., & Littleton, T. L. (1991). *Athletics and academe: An anatomy of abuses and a prescription for reform.* New York: Macmillan.

Barnhart, T. (1991, August 3). Knapp: Georgia won't compromise on academics. *The Atlanta Journal/The Atlanta Constitution,* pp. D1, D8.

Editor. (1991, August 6). This kind of 'cancer' doesn't help U. GA. *The Atlanta Constitution,* p. A8.

Falla, J. (1981). *NCAA: The voice of college sports.* Mission, KS: National Collegiate Athletic Association.

Gates, H. L., Jr. (1991, August 15). Delusions of grandeur. *Sports Illustrated*, p. 78.

Ingram, R. (1990, January 25). Quality education, Dorset tells prospects. *Birmingham News*, p. F6.

Knight Foundation Commission on Intercollegiate Athletics. (1991). *Keeping faith with the student athlete: A new model for intercollegiate athletics*. Charlotte, NC: Knight Foundation.

National Collegiate Athletic Association. (1991a). *NCAA academic performance study* (Report 91-02). Overland Park, KS: Author.

National Collegiate Athletic Association. (1991b). *NCAA manual*. Overland Park, KS: Author.

NCAA Academic Requirements Committee. (1991). Unpublished report to NCAA Presidents Commission.

Roberts, G. R. (1989). Racism, education, and intercollegiate athletics. *Sports Lawyer*, *7*, 9–10.

Smith, R. A. (1988). *Sports and freedom: The rise of big-time college athletics*. New York: Oxford University Press.

Whalen, J. S. (1991, August 14). Fickel factor frustrates Ithaca College president. *NCAA News*, p. 4.

CHAPTER 14

Controversies in Sports Medicine

KARL B. FIELDS AND MARTHA J. DELANEY

During the past decade dramatic successes in sports medicine have captured the imagination of the American public. Champions who overcome serious injuries become modern heroes. Electronic and printed media herald the rapid recovery of Olympic, professional, and collegiate athletes after career-threatening injury. This glorified view of medicine conquering adversity overshadows the reality that many injuries do profoundly affect the athlete's career. Also, traditional medical dogma has helped perpetuate some misconceptions that have kept women and athletes with medical illness from competing at the highest levels. Myths buttressed with medical legitimization do not fade easily. This chapter addresses myths and realities as they pertain to six areas of sports medicine. Understanding these can help the athlete, coach, educator, and health care professional to work together to ensure safer competition for all participants.

GENDER AND SPORT

Title 9 legislation in 1970 marked the entry of large numbers of female athletes into organized American sports. In the 1970s, female participation in high school sports increased by over 700% (Fields, 1988). Prior to this time diverse groups including Olympic organizers, athletic administrators, coaches, and physicians all played a role in limiting sports opportunities for women. Various groups perpetuated four prevalent myths regarding women in sports.

1. Women cannot safely participate in contact sports.
2. Women are more prone to injury than men.
3. Childbearing potential will be permanently impaired by vigorous sport.
4. Women cannot compete during menses.

Medical reports in the first few years after enactment of Title 9 tended to support the concerns raised about increased injury risks. However, as women have gained more experience in the techniques of different sports, as the quality of women's coaches and support staff have improved, and as physicians have learned to address women's specific health needs, injury rates among female athletes have declined. Injury risk now is considered sport-specific rather than gender-specific. Only injuries like stress fractures precipitated by bone loss from athletic amenorrhea remain substantially more common among women athletes (Barrow & Saha, 1988).

The entry of women into serious endurance sports, particularly distance running, dispelled the concerns about infertility from vigorous physical activity. The 1984 women's Olympic marathon champion and the world-record holder in the women's marathon both interrupted their racing careers to have children. Neither of these women experienced fertility problems, and both successfully returned to world-class competition after childbearing. Similarly, several women have disproved the notions regarding menses by candidly admitting that Olympic championship performances occurred during the peak of their menstrual cycles.

Only in the past 10 years have myths regarding women and sports begun to fade. Too often policies limiting female participation were based on opinions of male officials with little knowledge of or empathy for the female athlete. Sports medicine has helped establish the reality that male and female athletes share more similarities than differences. The future may see women entering essentially all sports played by men (see chapter 10).

MEDICAL ILLNESS AND SPORTS

A second group of individuals who faced exclusion from sports were athletes unfortunate enough to have a chronic illness. Two myths expressed the common thoughts that led to these limitations.

1. Patients with chronic illness should avoid competitive sports since this activity will hamper their ability to resist the disease.
2. Chronic illness lessens the physical capabilities of patients to such an extent that they should not expect championship-level performances.

Historically, certain observations established the bases of these myths. For example, asthma was first recognized as a breathing disorder by Aretaus in the second century A.D. Physicians through the ages noted that exercise worsened the symptoms of asthma. A logical conclusion seemed to be that avoidance of exercise would benefit asthmatics (Katz, 1987). Physicians drew similar conclusions from observed occurrences of sudden death during exercise in patients with illnesses as diverse as heart disease, diabetes, and epilepsy. These clinical observations led to the general exclusion of athletes with illness from all but the most nonstrenuous sports.

The 1984 Olympics helped dispel preconceived notions regarding asthma. Testing of the U.S. athletes revealed that 11.4% had either chronic asthma or exercise-induced asthma. These athletes accounted for 47 medals, which represented a better showing than that of the nonasthmatic athletes (Katz, 1987). Retesting of 1988 U.S. Olympic athletes revealed that about the same percentage was affected by asthma, proving that the earlier results were valid (American Academy of Pediatrics, 1989). Since this testing, numerous Olympic champions have helped spread the word about their success and about how sports helped lessen their problems with asthma (Hogshead & Couzens, 1990).

Similarly, a national panel of speakers who have been all-star professional athletes lectures about "winning with diabetes." Diabetic patients achieve better control of blood sugar, improved circulation, lower cardiovascular risks, and, perhaps most importantly, higher self-esteem through participation in sports. Other illnesses, including epilepsy, generally are easier to control in the physically active patient. Thus, the athletes themselves have demonstrated the beneficial effects of sports for chronic illness. Their success at all levels of competition speaks for itself.

SUDDEN DEATH, CARDIAC DISEASE, AND SPORTS

Tragedy in sports generates extremely emotional responses and often recriminations. All are struck by the inappropriateness of death in a young vital individual in quest of success in a game. Blame is directed toward coaches, officials, and often physicians. The lay public wants to believe a common myth about sudden cardiac death in young athletes:

1. Physicians can identify those competitors most likely to experience sudden death.

Coaches, athletic trainers, and numerous doctors also have trouble accepting the limitations of medicine's ability to identify the one athlete in 200,000 who is likely to die suddenly while competing (Epstein & Maron, 1986).

Two recent deaths of high-profile athletes underscore the difficulty in identifying unsuspected heart disease. Pete Maravich, a basketball player, had passed numerous physical evaluations from childhood until his untimely death at age 40. He managed to compete in one of the most strenuous sports at the highest collegiate and professional levels. Yet he died of a congenital coronary artery anomaly that had been present his entire lifetime. Since this condition had never caused him discomfort or limited his exercise capacity, no physician would have ordered a cardiac catheterization, the only test likely to lead to a proper diagnosis (Van Camp & Choi, 1988).

Flo Hyman became the star spiker for the U.S. Olympic women's volleyball team. After the Olympics she traveled to Japan to compete in professional volleyball. In a game no different than thousands she had played, she came to the sidelines, collapsed suddenly, and died at age 26. At autopsy physicians discovered that she had Marfan's syndrome. This congenital disorder is associated with unusual height, long arms, long fingers and toes, and a number of physical problems including a weakness in the aorta. The aorta, the major artery exiting from the heart, ruptured in Flo Hyman, leading to her sudden death.

Marfan's syndrome represents a clinical condition characterized by certain anatomical changes. However, many individuals with this condition have only a few of the stigmata. Thus, Flo Hyman looked no different from numerous other tall, thin competitors. Only an exceedingly astute physician would have thought to order an expensive test like an echocardiogram to detect an enlarged aorta. No other laboratory or radiologic tests would point to this diagnosis (Cantwell, 1986).

Currently, the reality of sudden cardiac death in young athletes is that rare congenital cardiac diseases cause most of these fatalities and no acceptable medical screens will identify the majority of the individuals likely to be affected (Lewis et al., 1989). Interestingly, this reality may one day become a myth, as recent cardiac deaths in young athletes relate more to cocaine usage and possibly to other dangerous practices such as anabolic steroid use or blood doping. These types of illegal practices may be lessened by better drug education and detection programs.

A second myth, this one regarding heart disease in older athletes, gained popularity among those most interested in running:

2. An athlete conditioned well enough to endure the rigors of a marathon run will not die from significant coronary atherosclerosis.

This myth originally carried the label of the "Bassler Hypothesis," because T. J. Bassler, MD, a pathologist, postulated that any athlete with major circulatory limitation would likely suffer breakdown of relatively avascular tissue like the Achilles tendon before developing the capacity to complete a marathon. Bassler noted that autopsies of marathon runners who had died suddenly revealed that even those with known heart disease had not died of coronary occlusion from atherosclerosis (Bassler, 1977a, 1977b). While Bassler correctly noted improved survival and lessening of disease in those cardiac patients who had become physically active, nothing in medicine is absolute. Certain runners develop a false sense of invulnerability and may ignore warning symptoms such as chest pain. The untimely heart attack death of Jim Fixx, the popular author of *The Complete Book of Running*, helped dispel this myth. Fixx had successfully completed a number of marathons and trained regularly until his death (Van Camp, 1988).

The reality is that numerous athletic individuals have died of coronary artery disease in spite of their outstanding level of physical fitness. Exercise reduces risks of cardiac disease but cannot reverse other cardiac risk factors such as family history, lipid abnormalities, history of smoking, hypertension, diabetes, and personality characteristics like hostility. Fortunately, exercise tolerance testing and other medical evaluation can promote early detection of high-risk athletes with coronary artery disease. In light of this capacity for early detection, dispelling the myth that fitness equals a healthy heart assumes added importance.

CONCUSSION AS A MINOR RISK IN SPORTS

The sports establishment has accepted that contact and collision sports pose a risk of head injury. Several myths still influence the approach to dealing with athletes who suffer a concussion.

1. Extent of injury can be determined by the degree of concussion.

This clinical observation comes from experience with catastrophic head injuries that were associated with significant loss of consciousness. Clearly, loss of consciousness indicates a potentially serious trauma that might involve brain damage. Unfortunately, the converse is not always true. For example, the athlete who experiences a mild concussion in which no loss of consciousness occurs (e.g., the football player who takes a hard hit and cannot remember what happened) cannot be confidently reassured that no serious brain trauma will result. These minor concussions in football are termed "bell-ringers" and are a frequent incident. Typically when the player clears his thinking in 20 to 30 seconds and has no physical problems he can return to the game (Kelly et al., 1991). However, a small percentage of these players with minimal symptoms have more serious problems, including intracranial bleeding. The reality in modern sports medicine is that Computerized Axial Tomography (CT) scans and Magnetic Resonance Imaging (MRI) have demonstrated that many seemingly innocuous accidents really pose considerable risk. Most athletes who have any degree of concussion in the future may require CT evaluation rather than the traditional clinical assessments that team physicians have used for years (Gentry, Godersky, & Thompson, 1988; Hesselink et al., 1988; Levin et al., 1987).

Another myth coming under challenge in the 1990s also relates to concussion:

2. Concussions rarely leave residual effects.

The clinical observation that headaches persist for weeks and sometimes longer following a concussion led to further assessment of brain function following minor head injury. Psychometric testing of individuals who had suffered concussions yielded troubling results. Performance on these tests declined from preinjury levels and sometimes stayed depressed for 3 months or longer. Whether these results indicate a long-term health risk to the injured person has not been determined (Levin et al., 1987).

Adding to concerns about the consequences of multiple minor head injuries is a clinical syndrome found in many retired boxers and known as "dementia pugilista." The syndrome is characterized by premature loss of normal central nervous system function. The cumulative effect of multiple blows to the head results in pathologic changes in brain substance even in boxers who experienced no "knockouts." Even with our sophisticated diagnostic tools, we cannot always predict the significance of head trauma or determine how many head impacts an athlete can safely sustain (Lampert & Hardman, 1984).

The uncertainty of the diagnosis in minor head injury and the lack of knowledge concerning the long-term sequelae add to the importance of research into prevention of head injuries. The reality of modern sports medicine suggests that neurological injury assessment will remain elusive for the foreseeable future. However, studies showing that helmet use reduces head injuries in equestrian sports, biking, and football all lend credence to the philosophy that "an ounce of prevention is worth a pound of cure" (Fields, 1989; Kraus, Anderson, & Mueller, 1970; Sacks, Holmgreen, Smith, & Sosin, 1991). Unfortunately, no head injury can really be regarded as minor, and avoidance is the only safe strategy.

ANABOLIC STEROID CONTROVERSIES

Ben Johnson's disqualification from the 1988 Olympics focused worldwide attention on the illegal use of anabolic steroids by athletes. Many years before this, though, their use in strength sports had become commonplace (Hallagan, Hallagan, & Snyder, 1989). The masculinization of women athletes from communist block countries aroused suspicions even in the 1960 and 1964 Olympics. Four myths contributed to the confusion surrounding anabolic steroid use and may have delayed the consensus necessary to implement regulation.

1. Steroids do not help.
2. Steroids always give the athlete an advantage.
3. Steroids frequently cause major medical complications.
4. Education of athletes will lead them to avoid steroid use.

Historically, anabolic steroids first were used by Hitler's Germany to make their infantry soldiers more aggressive. Chemists developed them from testosterone, and the masculinizing effects derive from a similarity to this hormone. Early studies in western nations showed mixed results and helped give birth to the myth that they did not help athletes develop strength. This became the position of the American College of Sports Medicine. The studies were done with miniscule doses compared to the regimens used by athletes and simply were not comparable. Athletes clearly could see results, and thus doctors lost credibility when they advised athletes that no scientific studies indicated that steroids would help them become stronger (Haupt & Rovere, 1984).

Athletes spread their own myths and perpetuated the idea that anabolic steroids always gave their users an advantage. The advice, and often the supply of the products, came from the "big man" in the gym. A dosage that worked for one individual often produced side effects in another. A second problem noted by a number of team physicians was an increase in injuries among users. Many competitors also experienced dramatic mood swings that interfered with the focus necessary for performance. The net result was that while steroids gave some athletes a competitive advantage, others found themselves unable to participate.

The third myth—that steroids frequently cause serious medical complications—arose from good-faith efforts by physicians to discourage their use. Physicians saw a biased sample of steroid-using athletes, since those with major complications sought medical care while a "silent majority" continued using the drugs without serious problems. Thus, as physicians "preached" of imminent danger, athletes had only to look around the locker room to see that the risks were overblown. For this reason physicians again lost credibility with athletes as a source of information regarding anabolic steroid use.

The reality is that steroids can put the user at risk for serious medical problems. These range from acceleration of arteriosclerosis to increased incidence of certain tumors to psychological breakdown. Fortunately, though, major problems strike only a small minority of users. Since this remains the case, most athletes choose to play the "Russian roulette" of steroid use in hopes of gaining the competitive advantage (Yesalis, Wright, & Lombardo, 1989).

Athletic administrators perpetuate the final myth—that better education will discourage athletes from using anabolic steroids. The irony of this approach stems from the fact that athletes tend to have more knowledge regarding anabolic steroid use and its effects than do many health care professionals. Contrary to popular belief, most athletes are well-educated, success-oriented individuals who estimate the risks of steroid use and weigh them against the potential advantages. The lure of the fame, fortune, and adulation that accompany elite athlete status simply outweighs the concern about harm. Second, many athletes begin steroid use in late adolescence, a developmental phase of life during which the individual often feels immortal.

The reality of anabolic steroid control lies more with testing and regulation than with physicians or educators. The United States Olympic Committee, recognizing this, imposes strict sanctions ranging from temporary suspension for first-time anabolic steroid users to permanent disqualification for repeat offenders (Voy, 1988). The general consensus is that since track and field implemented widespread testing and imposed a number of disqualifications, usage has declined. Interestingly, in the past year only one shotputter was able to consistently throw for a distance greater than 70 feet, whereas that distance was commonly obtained in previous years. Other drops in performances suggest by implication that usage has decreased. Similarly, the NCAA and professional football leagues have recently redirected efforts to stress that anabolic steroids are illegal drugs and that positive steroid tests will result in penalties (see chapter 15).

PSYCHOLOGICAL FACTORS IN INJURY

Much of sports medicine has focused on the orthopedic components of injury. In essence medicine has perpetuated the following myth:

Most injuries relate primarily to physical factors.

Clinical observations that patients with unusual leg alignment, high arches, lack of flexibility, or weakness frequently come to doctors' offices for treatment support the idea that anatomical problems cause injury. However, of these physical changes only muscular weakness has convincingly been demonstrated as a clear causal factor in injury. Research has not yet defined the prevalence of many other changes in athletes, so the amount of increased risk attributed to a specific physical change cannot confidently be estimated.

None of the theories regarding anatomical problems sufficiently explains the phenomenon that many coaches refer to as the "injury-prone" athlete. Interestingly, limited studies suggest that psychological factors may predispose athletes to problems. Considering football and other contact or collision sports, a plausible explanation may be that increased risk-taking behaviors in late adolescence lead to injuries. Injury statistics demonstrate that athletes ages 16 and 17 experience higher injury rates than their younger counterparts, even when the figures are adjusted to account for their higher playing time (Garrick, 1990). Another study shows higher injury rates in football players from dysfunctional families (Coddington & Troxell, 1980). Perhaps family problems or other causes of emotional stress affect the athlete's impulse control and lead to unsafe actions. Additional support for the theory that psychological factors promote injury comes from a small study of runners. Runners with high Type A behavior scores showed a markedly elevated risk for multiple injuries (Fields, Delaney, & Hinkle, 1990).

The reality of current sports medicine knowledge regarding the causes of injury is that little is known. Clinical suspicions have pointed to likely problems including physical and psychological factors. Small-scale studies support certain theories, but until more extensive research is completed physicians cannot confidently explain injury causality.

CONCLUSION

Athletes compete during years of dramatic physical and psychological growth. Often they need to seek both medical and emotional support from sports medicine specialists. Advances in sports medicine over the past decade have in each of the six areas discussed in this chapter dispelled myths that prevent athletes from receiving the best advice for sports participation. Historically, coaches, educators, administrators, parents, fellow athletes, the media, and the medical establishment have all played a role in perpetuating the misconceptions. When physicians give inaccurate information (such as has been the case with anabolic steroids), they lose their credibility among athletes. Sports medicine specialists must strive to provide objective, unemotional advice in a nonjudgmental fashion. Preconceived notions about gender, race, or disability must not be used to limit participation. Myths develop quickly in sports lore, but unfortunately establishing reality takes many years.

References

American Academy of Pediatrics, Section on Allergy and Immunology, Section on Diseases of the Chest. (1989). Exercise and the asthmatic child. *Pediatrics, 84*(2), 392–393.

Barrow, G. W., & Saha, S. (1988). Menstrual irregularity and stress fractures in collegiate female distance runners. *American Journal of Sports Medicine, 16*(3), 209–216.

Bassler, T. J. (1977a). Marathon running and immunity to atherosclerosis. *Annals of New York Academy of Sciences, 301*, 579–592.

Bassler, T. J. (1977b, July). Parallel aging of Achilles tendon and coronary artery. *British Medical Journal, 2*(6081), 262–263.

Cantwell, J. D. (1986). Marfan's syndrome: Detection and management. *Physician and Sports Medicine, 14*(7), 51–55.

Coddington, R. D., & Troxell, J. R. (1980). The effect of emotional factors on football injury rates: A pilot study. *Journal of Human Stress, 6*(4), 3–5.

Epstein, S. E., & Maron, B. J. (1986). Sudden death and the competitive athlete: Perspectives on preparticipation screening studies. *Journal of the American College of Cardiology, 7*(1), 220–230.

Fields, K. B. (1988). Assessing sports related injuries. In P. D. Sloane, L. M. Slatt, & R. M. Baker (Eds.), *Essentials of family medicine* (pp. 260–266). Baltimore, MD: Williams and Wilkins.

Fields, K. B. (1989). Head injuries in soccer. *Physician and Sports Medicine, 17*(1), 72–73.

Fields, K. B., Delaney, M. J., & Hinkle, J. S. (1990). A prospective study of Type A behavior and running injuries. *Journal of Family Practice, 30*(4), 425–429.

Garrick, J. G. (1990). Epidemiology of sports injuries in the pediatric athlete. In J. A. Sullivan & W. A. Grana (Eds.), *The pediatric athlete* (pp. 123–132). Park Ridge, IL: American Academy of Orthopaedic Surgeons.

Gentry, L. R., Godersky, J. C., & Thompson, B. (1988). MR imaging of head trauma: Review of the distribution and radiopathologic features of traumatic lesions. *American Journal of Roentgenology, 150*, 663–672.

Hallagan, J. B., Hallagan, L. F., & Snyder, M. B. (1989). Anabolic-androgenic steroid use by athletes. *New England Journal of Medicine, 321*(15), 1042–1045.

Haupt, H. A., & Rovere, G. D. (1984). Anabolic steroids: A review of the literature. *American Journal of Sports Medicine, 12*(6), 469–484.

Hesselink, J. R., Dowd, C. F., Healy, M. E., Hajek, P., Baker, L. L., & Luerssen, T. G. (1988). MR imaging of brain contusions: A comparative study with CT. *American Journal of Roentgenology, 150,* 1133–1142.

Hogshead, N., & Couzens, G. S. (1990). *Asthma and exercise.* New York: Henry Holt and Company.

Katz, R. M. (1987). Coping with exercise-induced asthma in sports. *Physician and Sports Medicine, 15*(7), 101–108.

Kelly, J. P., Nichols, J. S., Filley, C. M., Lillehei, K. O., Rubinstein, D., & Kleinschmidt-DeMasters, B. K. (1991). Concussion in sports: Guidelines for the prevention of catastrophic outcome. *Journal of the American Medical Association, 266,* 2867–2869.

Kraus, J. F., Anderson, B. D., & Mueller, C. E. (1970). An investigation of the effectiveness of a new helmet to control touch football head injuries. *American Journal of Public Health, 60*(5), 903–912.

Lampert, P. W., & Hardman, J. M. (1984). Morphological changes in brains of boxers. *Journal of the American Medical Association, 251*(20), 2676–2679.

Levin, H. S., Amparo, E., Eisenberg, H. M., Williams, D. H., High, W. M., McArdle, C. B., & Weiner, R. L. (1987). Magnetic resonance imaging and computerized tomography in relation to the neurobehavioral sequelae of mild and moderate head injuries. *Journal of Neurosurgery, 66,* 706–713.

Lewis, J. F., Maron, B. J., Diggs, J. A., Spencer, J. E., Mehrotra, P. P., & Curry, C. L. (1989). Preparticipation echocardiographic screening for cardiovascular disease in a large, predominantly Black population of collegiate athletes. *American Journal of Cardiology, 64,* 1029–1033.

Sacks, J. J., Holmgreen, P., Smith, S. M., & Sosin, D. M. (1991). Bicycle-associated head injuries and deaths in the United States from 1984 through 1988. *Journal of the American Medical Association, 226*(21), 3016–3018.

Van Camp, S. P. (1988). Exercise-related sudden death: Risks and causes (Part 1). *Physician and Sports Medicine, 16*(5), 97, 99, 103–105, 107–109, 112.

Van Camp, S. P., & Choi, J. H. (1988). Exercise and sudden death. *Physician and Sports Medicine, 16*(3), 49, 52.

Voy, R. O. (1988). *United States Olympic Committee Division of Sports Medicine and Science guide to banned medications* (pp. 1–15). Colorado Springs, CO: U.S. Olympic Committee.

Yesalis, C. E., Wright, J. E., Lombardo, J. A. (1989). Anabolic-androgenic steroids: A synthesis of existing data and recommendations for future research. *Clinical Sports Medicine, 1*(3), 109–134.

CHAPTER 15

Law and Sports

GEORGE W. SCHUBERT AND ARLINE F. SCHUBERT

Litigation in amateur sports has increased dramatically during the past 10 years. Numerous institutions, including law schools, presently offer specialized courses in sports law. Contrary to what many believe, institutions of higher education can and will be sued. Lawsuits arise when communication with the student athlete or the parents or guardians breaks down or when the administrator working with the student athlete does not follow the university's procedures and policies.

The purpose of this chapter is to introduce and to discuss briefly the topic of law and collegiate sports, thereby possibly preventing litigation in the areas discussed. However, individuals working with student athletes ideally should not comply with the law merely out of fear of lawsuits. Rather, they should look at the positive aspects of adhering to the law. By adhering to the law in counseling student athletes, the counselor will help the student have a positive growth experience and set an ethical pattern for the student. In this chapter, basic information, recent research, and a brief analysis is presented on each of the following topics: negligence, due process, gender discrimination and equal opportunity, drug testing, agents, and the National Letter of Intent. It is important that sports administrators confront the numerous realities of litigation in all areas of sports activity. Lawsuits are disruptive to the educational mission of the institution and consume money and other resources that could be put to better use.

NEGLIGENCE

As a general rule, courts have held that student athletes assume the risks that are incidental to participation. Unless the coach, league, or school is shown to have acted negligently, the injured student athlete will not recover from the athletic director, coach, league, or school for injuries resulting from participation in a sport (*Nydegger v. Don Bosco Preparatory High School*, 1985). In order to prevent potential liability, then, the administrator of the athletic program must develop and implement strategies to reduce the risk of injuries.

Negligence is defined as the lack of due care under the circumstances. If an injured party can prove that an individual who is responsible acted in a manner or failed to act and that either of these behaviors caused an injury, then liability will be found based upon negligence. For example, an institution must adequately train or coach the athletes. Also, a coach must warn participants of inherently dangerous equipment, and a failure to make such warnings may result in liability (*Kirk v. Washington State University*, 1987). It is sufficient proof of negligence when a plaintiff introduces evidence which would lead a reasonable person to conclude that the event or injury was caused by the coach's not properly training, supervising, or informing the student athlete (*Hornyak v. Promfret School*, 1986).

Coaches must be alert to all safety recommendations of the various sports. For example, in the first few days of practice any student athlete who does not have the proper uniform and equipment should not compete in agility drills where contact is inherent. The student who does not receive the proper equipment necessary to participate cannot assume the risk of injury (*Leahy v. School Board of Hernando County*, 1984).

Coaches must take ordinary care in the inspection and distribution of athletic equipment designed to protect players from injury. If the coach does not take ordinary care in the inspection of equipment issued to student athletes, the coach will not be able to successfully defend against a lawsuit by asserting that the athlete assumed the risk (*Thomas v. Chicago Board of Education*, 1978).

Sometimes a student athlete is injured by another student athlete. In such a case, the injured athlete can recover damages only if it can be shown that the opponent acted with reckless disregard of the injured party's safety (*Oswald v. Township High School District, No. 214*, 1980). The court in *Nobozny v. Barnhill* (1975) was careful to emphasize the fact that if a game involves contact, the responsibility of the individual in charge will be greater than when the game does not involve contact. The court added that the legal system should not impose unreasonable responsibilities upon individuals who participate actively in sports.

In cases where a participant is injured, but ordinary care and common sense on the part of the injured participant would have prevented the injury, the coach, league, and institution will not be held liable. But there are exceptions. For example, if a player is injured, the injured player may sue the team doctor or trainer. If the doctor and/or the trainer knew (or should have known) that the injured party was weak from an illness, previously injured, or currently taking prescribed medication for an existing condition, the injured participant may claim that the doctor or trainer acted recklessly or willfully in utter disregard of the welfare of the injured participant.

The claim of reckless or willful disregard for the welfare of the athlete will overcome the defense of ordinary care and the defense of governmental immunity (*Sorey v. Kellett*, 1988). Governmental (or sovereign) immunity has been a traditional defense used by state agencies. However, this defense has been controlled by legislation. In some states legislators have enacted laws which abolish this defense, and in other states legislators have said that if liability insurance is purchased by an agency of the state the student athlete suffering injury may seek damages up to the maximum limit of the insurance coverage (*Overcash v. Statesville City Board of Education*, 1986). Some institutions do purchase disability insurance; however, they are not required by law to do so.

DUE PROCESS

It is important for the counselor or administrator who is advising the student athlete to be aware of the student athlete's rights. The student athlete may not have a right to a scholarship, but once a scholarship is received, the student athlete is deserving of some due process if the scholarship is to be revoked. Due process is the right to a hearing before an action occurs. The student athlete who "loses" a scholarship should be informed of the reasons for the revocation.

During recent years, particularly the past 5, providing due process for athletic personnel has become extremely important. National leaders have proposed federal legislation that calls for the use of due process by the National Collegiate Athletic Association (NCAA) (Lederman, 1991). Numerous states, including California, Florida, Illinois, Iowa, Kansas, Minnesota, Nebraska, Nevada, New York, and South Carolina, have proposed or passed state legislation that will require that due process procedures be followed regarding athletic matters (Lederman, 1991; "Lobbying Groups," 1991).

The Fifth Amendment to the United States Constitution provides for federal procedural due process. It states, "No person shall be deprived of life, liberty, or property, without due process of law; . . ." The Fourteenth Amendment to the United States Constitution provides for procedural due process at the state level. This amendment states, "No state shall . . . deprive any person of life, liberty, or property, without due process of law; . . ." Procedural due process limitations on state activity are also found in state constitutions. Therefore, one must examine the individual state law as well as the Fifth and Fourteenth Amendments to the United States Constitution. For a party who has alleged a violation of property right and chooses to use the Fourteenth Amendment equal protection clause to prevail, that claimant must prove that state action is involved in the violation. The claimant must also show that differential treatment exists. Once state action and differential treatment have been established, the claimant must show that the alleged violation does not have a substantial relationship to a legitimate governmental objective (Schubert-Madsen & Schubert, 1989).

At the inception of a collegiate athletic career, the student athlete does not have a constitutional right to participate in collegiate athletics or to receive athletic grant-in-aid. Courts have stated that a property interest does not exist under the Constitution (*Goss v. Lopez*, 1975). As factors are introduced into the student athlete's career, however, this may change. The right that the student athlete seeks is a property right, and if the property right can be proved, then due process must be forthcoming. Courts have held that in order to prevail in an action based on due process arguments, the party alleging the complaint must state and prove a property interest.

Courts have not agreed that because a student athlete participates on an athletic team and has an athletic scholarship the student athlete has a property interest. When this issue has been raised in the past, courts have determined that the complaining party is dealing only with athletics, and that is one component of the educational package rather than the entire educational process. Questions have arisen concerning the right to participate in athletics, the right to athletic scholarships, the right to be viewed by the public as an athlete, and numerous other rights. Student athletes have consistently maintained, and a few courts have agreed, that there is a right to procedural due process when a student athlete has begun participation in college athletics or has received an athletic grant-in-aid (Schubert-Madsen & Schubert, 1989). Most courts, however, have held that this property right generally extends to high school student athletes because state laws provide entitlement to a high school education, but this entitlement does not extend to a collegiate student athlete. One may argue that free tuition to a university may be similarly compared to the free education received by those students in high school. If so, why is there no entitlement to due process at the university for a student athlete similar to the due process provided to high school students? This may be answered by the courts' refusal to focus on the specific issue of a fundamental right. Courts will protect an individual's right of access to an education and will review any systems that seem to deny educational benefits because of suspect criteria, which include discrimination based on race, religion, or sex. The right to free education entitles one to an education, but not the right to participate on an athletic team.

GENDER DISCRIMINATION AND EQUAL OPPORTUNITY

Historically, men and women have been separated in many activities and organizations based upon gender differences. However, in 1961, President John F. Kennedy issued an executive order establishing the President's Commission on the Status of Women. From the Commission's findings and congressional hearings it became evident that gender discrimination was rampant in this country (Schubert-Madsen, Schubert, & Schubert, 1991).

In 1988 the NCAA Committee on Women's Athletics requested that the NCAA member institutions be surveyed as to women's perceptions of the barriers they encounter in pursuit of careers in college athletics. Ninety-three percent of the female administrators surveyed indicated that "old-boy networking" was a factor which negatively affected women in administrative positions. Only 5.3% of female student athletes surveyed reported that they would seek a position in intercollegiate athletics immediately following graduation. Ninety percent of the female coaches surveyed reported that the salary was inadequate relative to the time commitment necessary to coaching. Eighty-nine percent of the female coaches surveyed agreed that women coaches provide role models and guidance for women athletes in ways that men cannot ("Women's Athletics," 1991).

States have separated male and female athletes due to the physical differences between the sexes. This has been done for two reasons: First, it was, and to some extent still is, believed that there may be more physical danger to a female athlete who is competing in a contact sport that includes male athletes than to a female athlete competing solely against other female athletes. Second, there is a belief that if male and female athletes were allowed to compete against each other, male athletes would dominate the athletic programs and deny female athletes the opportunity to participate. States have promulgated rules prohibiting male athletes from participating on female teams, and legal actions have been brought by male athletes who wanted to participate on those teams. Such segregation is subject to scrutiny under the equal protection clause of the Fourteenth Amendment. In order for the classification by gender to be constitutional, it must have a rational relationship to a valid state purpose.

If an institution demonstrates that there is potential harm to the female student athlete—or to the male student athlete—due to the nature of the contact sport in question, it will be allowed to limit participation in that sport on the basis of gender, because safeguarding the students' welfare is a viable state objective. The state must show that its primary concern is for the health and safety of participants.

Individuals who believe that they have been victims of gender-based discrimination usually depend on the Fourteenth Amendment of the United States Constitution and on Title IX of the Education Amendment of 1972 for assistance. In addition, in 1988 the United States Congress passed the Civil Rights Restoration Act. This Act states that all programs and activities of an institution are subject to federal antidiscrimination laws if any federal aid is received by the institution in any one of its programs or activities (Public Law No. 100-259, 1988).

Courts have emphasized that institutions may provide separate programs for men and women. However, programs must exist for both genders, and there must be an opportunity for both to participate in athletics (Schubert, Schubert, & Schubert-Madsen, 1991). Separatism is not usually the issue. Rather, the issue is one of equality. A party seeking to uphold a statute that classifies individuals on the basis of their gender must carry the burden of showing an extremely persuasive justification for the classification. This burden is met by showing that the classification serves an important governmental objective.

DRUG TESTING

Courts have held that to test the general student population for drugs by the use of urine samples constitutes a search. Courts have determined that such searches violate the individual's Fourth Amendment right of freedom from unreasonable search and seizure, as well as the right to legitimate expectation of privacy and personal security ensured by the First Amendment (*Anable v. Ford*, 1985). It has also been held that random drug testing of the general student population violates the due process clause of the Fourteenth Amendment (*Odenheim v. Carlstadt, East Rutherford Regional School District*, 1985).

On the other hand, testing that is limited to potential interscholastic sports participants has been determined to be constitutional where the tests are limited in scope, provide for student privacy, and clearly state the consequences of positive tests. When an individual has diminished expectations of privacy and where the governmental interest is significantly important, the searches via urinalysis are constitutional. If an institution requires the student athlete to sign a form indicating consent to testing for prohibited drugs prior to participation, there is a diminished expectation of privacy. If a student athlete consents to testing, the consent must be voluntary and the student athlete must know the consequences of signing the consent agreement. Also, most locker rooms are communal, and this reduces the expectation of privacy even more (*Schaill v. Tippecanoe County School Corporation*, 1988).

The *NCAA Manual* states that a student athlete who is found to have utilized a substance on the list of banned drugs shall be declared ineligible for further participation in postseason and regular season competition until one calendar year after the positive drug test and until the student athlete retests negative and his or her eligibility is restored by the NCAA executive committee (NCAA, 1991). A federal district court in the State of Washington determined that the NCAA's requirement that a student athlete sign a consent-to-testing form prior to participating in the sport was not unconstitutional. The court weighed the NCAA's interest in keeping intercollegiate athletics free from drugs with the hardship to the student of missing one season of competition and ruled that the NCAA's interest was greater than the interest of the individual student athlete (*O'Halloran v. University of Washington*, 1988). That same court ruled that the taking of the urine sample was not an unreasonable search. In *O'Halloran* (1988) the court stated clearly that participating in athletics at the college level is a privilege, that institutions may deny intercollegiate eligibility under certain circumstances, and that one of those circumstances was the with-holding of consent to the testing. The NCAA's interest in protecting the integrity of intercollegiate athletics outweighed the student athlete's privacy interest (*Bally v. Northeastern University*, 1989; *O'Halloran v. University of Washington*, 1988).

However, an appellate court in California determined that the NCAA-mandated drug tests for student athletes at Stanford University did violate the California constitutional right of privacy. Two student athletes who challenged the drug testing alleged that the tests were degrading and humiliating and incapable of measuring factors relevant to the athlete's performance. The NCAA argued that the Association needed the drug testing in order to protect the health and safety of student athletes and to protect the integrity of the athletes who participated in NCAA-sanctioned sporting events.

The appellate court ruled against the NCAA, pointing out that it had failed to show that drugs were, in fact, abused by student athletes. The court held that in the absence of a verified need for drug testing, the NCAA testing program did violate a student athlete's right of privacy. The trial court found no evidence that drug use in athletic contests was impairing the health or safety of the student athletes who were competing. The trial court also determined that there was no evidence that any college athlete had ever been injured in competition as a result of drug use. The court held that the NCAA drug testing program violated the privacy guaranteed by the California Constitution because it was overbroad ("Stanford Wins Another," 1991).

The student athlete may abuse over-the-counter drugs or prescribed medicines. Anabolic steroid use, once primarily a problem of professional athletes, has now trickled down to the high school level. Teens who want to look like the "pro wrestler" or the "pro lineman" use steroids to increase their muscle size. Impatience and desire to impress have created a crisis situation. The findings of an investigation and study performed in 1990 and released by Charles Yesalis and others at Penn State indicate that the abuse of synthetic anabolic steroids has reached epidemic proportions in the teenage male. The study indicates that the number of abusers, those who use the drug or steroid without medical advice, is in excess of 500,000 ("War on Steroids," 1990). To help wage a war on the illegal use of steroids, federal legislation has now been passed which places androgenic-anabolic compounds (steroids) in the classification of a controlled substance ("War on Steroids," 1990). In addition, in 1991 several states initiated legislation which would bring their states into conformance with federal law ("State Legislation," 1991).

Student athletes' drug problems and alcohol problems are no different from those of other students, except that student athletes are placed in stressful situations which can exacerbate the effects of drug and alcohol use. The student athlete is under tremendous pressure to succeed. As a result, the student athlete may resort to pain killers, steroids, or other drugs to alleviate pain or to enhance endurance.

AGENTS

The *NCAA Manual* states that "an individual shall be ineligible for participation in an intercollegiate sport if he or she ever has agreed (orally or in writing) to be represented by an agent for the purpose of marketing his or her athletic ability or reputation in that sport" (NCAA, 1991). Furthermore, the manual states that if the agreement, oral or written, is silent as to the particular sport, the individual will be ineligible for any sport (NCAA, 1991).

This area of sports law has been targeted by several states whose legislators have deemed it necessary to control the sports agent. In the 1980s 24 states promulgated legislation affecting the sports agent (Ehrhardt & Rodgers, 1988). This legislation reaffirmed the NCAA's position that collegiate athletes should not be compensated for their feats in the athletic arena. The legislation holds both the sports agent and the athlete accountable for violations.

Generally, an agent is described as "an individual authorized by another to act on his account and under his control" (Restatement [Second] of Agency Comment, 1958). The agent does not need any particular training or skill. Anyone can be an agent. However, the individual who decides to become an agent should have some abilities to negotiate and an understanding of the collective bargaining process. In addition, the agent must be skilled as a financial advisor and/or planner. A knowledgeable agent understands the market for athletes in a sport.

Athletes hire an agent to negotiate a professional contract (employment agreement) and to secure and negotiate commercial opportunities. The agent may assist the athlete in financial planning and management and provide counsel on tax matters. In the past, athletes found that they were unable to compete with the professional negotiator at the bargaining table. Athletes discovered that they were at a distinct disadvantage when salaries were determined and that an agent's representation was advisable.

In order to be protected and to have an equal advantage, athletes hired individuals who were allegedly skilled at negotiating an employment agreement. In reality athletes were wooed, wined, and dined by would-be agents who may not have had the requisite skills to be effective as agents. Athletes were given expensive gifts and loans if they would agree to be represented by the giver (*Walters v. Fullwood*, 1987).

This phenomenon created havoc at the NCAA central office. The NCAA promulgated regulations which prevented agents from offering inducements to college athletes and regulations which prevented agents from signing the athletes early. Section 12.3, "Use of Agents," in the *NCAA Manual* (1991) addresses the rules as they have been promulgated by members of the rules committee of the NCAA. In the rules it is clearly stated that the agreement with an agent does not have to be in writing (NCAA, 1991). The athlete cannot enter into any agreement to be represented by an agent while participating in the sport in which the student athlete will seek a professional contract. Neither the athlete nor the athlete's family can accept anything from an agent, because to do so is to take advantage of a benefit not available to the general student body (NCAA, 1991).

The student athlete may seek advice from either an attorney or a career counseling panel. However, the attorney cannot then attend a negotiating session with the athlete. If the attorney does attend a negotiating session, that attorney is then considered an agent. If a career counseling panel is used, it should have three members, of which only one can be a staff member of the athletic department, and the chief executive of the institution must disclose this panel to the NCAA national office (NCAA, 1991).

NATIONAL LETTER OF INTENT

The National Letter of Intent (NLI) is an agreement between a prospective student athlete (and his or her parent or legal guardian) and an NCAA member institution that has elected to subscribe to the NLI. The development of the NLI began in the early 1960s. The motivation behind the NLI is to reduce recruiting time, thereby reducing the institution's recruiting expenses. In addition, the NLI helps alleviate stress for the prospective student athlete and the athlete's family, and reduces the pressure on the athletic recruiter.

The NLI is a voluntary, cooperative program operated through the Collegiate Commissioners Association, which is made up of commissioners from various conferences. Conference member institutions participate through their respective conference offices, while independent institutions generally participate through the most appropriate conference commissioner, usually the conference located nearest the independent institution. Since the program is voluntary, it is dependent upon the member institutions for enforcement and success. Enforcement and questions regarding recruiting and the NLI are handled through the Collegiate Commissioners Association.

The NLI is intended for the prospective student athlete who will be entering a 4-year institution for the first time and for the prospective student athlete who is about to graduate from a junior college. In order to be eligible to sign an NLI, and in order for the NLI to be enforceable, the student must be offered financial aid from the institution and must meet the institution's admission requirements.

Any prospective student athlete who will be entering a 4-year institution for the first time as a full-time student is eligible to sign the NLI. Each prospective student athlete may sign only one NLI. However, if a prospective student athlete is a junior college transfer student, then it is possible that two NLIs will be signed—one prior to enrollment at the junior college and one prior to enrollment at the 4-year institution.

When the NLI is signed by the prospective student athlete, the institution is committed to the signee in the following ways: The student must receive in writing an award or recommendation for athletic grant-in-aid from the soliciting institution at the time of the signing, and that offer or recommendation must list the terms and conditions of the award, including the amount and duration of the financial assistance. Typically, an award letter for athletic grant-in-aid is submitted with the NLI. The award letter represents the institution's declaration of intent to award financial assistance to the prospective student athlete. In most instances, the institution commits itself to a financial award for a period of one academic year (two semesters or three quarters). The duration for the financial award is to be clearly specified on the financial assistance award letter.

The NLI commits the student to the institution for a period of one year. If the student wishes to transfer to another institution after the NLI has been signed or after the completion of an athletic and academic term at the first institution, penalties may be imposed. The basic penalty to the student who enrolls in another institution which participates in the NLI program is forfeiture of two seasons of intercollegiate athletic competition. The student will not be permitted to represent the latter institution in intercollegiate athletics until two full academic years of residence have been completed. However, the student and the institution holding the NLI may agree to a mutual release from the NLI; in such an instance, the student is ineligible for competition for a period of only one year and forfeits only one season of competition.

A coach at a member institution that subscribes to the NLI does not have the authority to release a student from the obligation. The institution is the obligated body, and the student must procure the mutual release from the institution, not the coach. Additionally, if a coach leaves an institution after the NLI has been signed the student athlete is still bound by the NLI until a mutual release from the institution is obtained. The NCAA rules which apply to the NLI are the same for Divisions I and II. Division III does not utilize the NLI (NCAA, 1991).

It should be noted that the NLI has never been litigated. Some probable reasons for this absence of litigation in a litigious society are as follows: (a) being involved with the NLI is voluntary; (b) the specific regulations and procedures pertaining to the document are clearly stated; and (c) the entire document is self-contained within four pages.

At least two aspects of the NLI appear to be susceptible to legal challenge. First, the requirement of the signature of a parent or legal guardian on the letter seems unenforceable, especially when the student athlete is over 18 years of age. Second, and probably more important, is the loss of two seasons of athletic eligibility when the letter is signed and then the student does not attend the institution to which the person is committed. The second legal challenge would be to argue that the penalty, which is the loss of two seasons of eligibility, is too severe.

CONCLUSION

Today more individuals are participating in sports and sports-related activities. As a result of the increased emphasis on sports, unnecessary risks are taken in order to win. The reality is that many coaches take unnecessary risks by using unsafe equipment, tired or injured athletes, and unusually dangerous plays. Student athletes also sometimes take unnecessary chances by participating in athletic events when they are ill or in a weakened condition. Or, they may rely on the use of drugs to stimulate their play or to enhance their physical growth.

Sports-related litigation has risen significantly in the past decade. Even though courts have been reluctant to find athletic personnel liable for physical injuries suffered by a player who voluntarily participates in an athletic event, athletic personnel must be aware that courts are at times inconsistent in their decisions. Also, the belief that collegiate athletic programs cannot or will not be sued is not based in reality. Athletic directors, coaches, and other athletic personnel responsible for the administration of the athletic program must become cognizant of the laws and changes in the laws which apply to athletics, or they will likely be involved in litigation. Probably, the best example of current changes in laws that affect coaches, student athletes, and athletic administrators is the increase in the amount of due process which must be afforded to individuals participating in established athletic programs before actions and penalties can be applied.

References

Anable v. Ford, 653 F. Supp. 22 (W.D. Ark. 1985).

Bally v. Northeastern University, 532 N.E.2d 49 (Mass. 1989).

Ehrhardt, C. W., & Rodgers, J. M. (1988). Tightening the defense against offensive sports agents. *Florida State University Law Review, 16*(3), 633.

Goss v. Lopez, 419 U.S. 565, 95 S. Ct. 729, 42 L.Ed.2d 725 (1975).

Hornyak v. Promfret School, 783 F.2d 284 (1st Cir. 1986).

Kirk v. Washington State University, 746 P.2d 285 (Wash. 1987).

Leahy v. School Board of Hernando County, 450 So.2d 883 (Fla. App. 5th Dist. 1984).

Lederman, D. (1991, June 26). Two coaches join with lawmakers to fight NCAA. *Chronicle of Higher Education,* p. 1, 26.

Lobbying groups continue efforts against the NCAA. (1991, July 31). *NCAA News,* pp. 10–11.

National Collegiate Athletic Association. (1991). *NCAA manual.* Overland Park, KS: Author.

Nobozny v. Barnhill, 334 N.E.2d 258 (Ill. 1975).

Nydegger v. Don Bosco Preparatory High School, 495 A.2d 485 (N.J. Super. 1985).

Odenheim v. Carlstadt, East Rutherford Regional School District, 510 A.2d 709 (N.J. Super. Ck. Div. 1985).

O'Halloran v. University of Washington, 679 F. Supp. 997 (W.D. Wash. 1988).

Oswald v. Township High School District, No. 214, 406 N.E.2d 157 (Ill. 1980).

Overcash v. Statesville City Board of Education, 348 S.E.2d 524 (N.C. App. 1986).

Public Law Number 100-259, 102, Stat. 28, (1988).

Restatement (Second) of Agency Comment (1958).

Schaill v. Tippecanoe County School Corporation, 864 F.2d 1309 (7th Cir. 1988).

Schubert, A. F., Schubert, G. W., & Schubert-Madsen, C. L. (1991). Changes influenced by litigation in women's intercollegiate athletics. *Seton Hall Journal of Sports Law, 1,* 235–266.

Schubert-Madsen, C. L., Schubert, A. F., & Schubert, G. W. (1991). Gender discrimination in athletics. *The North Dakota Law Review, 67,* 227.

Schubert-Madsen, C. L., & Schubert, G. W. (1989, Spring). The student-athlete: Procedural due process and property right. *The Academic Athletic Journal,* 31–38.

Sorey v. Kellett, 849 F.2d 960 (5th Cir. 1988).

Stanford wins another round in court on drug tests. (1991, October 1). *NCAA News,* p. 1.

State legislation relating to athletes. (1991, May 29). *NCAA News,* p. 23.

Thomas v. Chicago Board of Education, 377 N.E.2d 55 (Ill. App. 1st Dist. 1978).

Walters v. Fullwood, 675 F. Supp. 155 (S.D.N.Y. 1987).

War on steroids must be fought on several fronts. (1990, December 19). *NCAA News,* p. 4.

Women's athletics survey published. (1991, June 12). *NCAA News,* p. 1.

CASE STUDIES

Opportunites for Discussion

WYATT D. KIRK, SARAH V. KIRK, AND CONTRIBUTORS

The following seven composite cases are presented to demonstrate the variety and complexity of the problems experienced by student athletes as they strive to achieve the highest level of excellence through athletics. The cases illustrate some of the problematic experiences discussed in various chapters of this book. These cases are not necessarily typical scenarios and are not representative of all student athletes. Rather, they should be considered as study practice cases, from which one can gain insights into the interrelatedness of academics, athletics, discipline, and self-motivation as they affect the student athlete. Closely analyzed, the cases reveal a vast array of problems, changes, adaptations, and actions faced by student athletes. It is hoped that these illustrations will lead readers to think about how they can work effectively with this special population of students.

CASE STUDY *by Wayne Lanning and Peter Toye*

COUNSELING ATHLETES IN HIGHER EDUCATION

Tom appeared in our office midway through the 1990 football season. He was a redshirt sophomore running back (third year academically, second year of athletic eligibility) and complained of "just being down all the time and not caring about anything anymore."

History

Tom is a White, scholarshiped football player. His home was a large city in the midwest, where he starred in football, basketball, and track. He was named to numerous prestigious all-star teams in football and was recruited heavily in that sport. Tom's promising college football career had been jeopardized by a series of minor injuries beginning in his first year with the program. The 1990 season was supposed to be his time to begin making positive contributions to the team, but he was getting very little playing time. Tom missed the 1990 spring practice due to minor knee surgery. He was a solid "B" student throughout his first 2 years at the university.

Intervention

We met regularly for approximately 1 month. His presenting problem was a generalized feeling of depression marked by a lack of interest and energy relative to things that previously were of great importance to him, namely football and school. Tom's midterm grades were suffering, and he was questioning whether he wanted to continue to play football because it was no longer "fun."

As we discussed his situation, it became apparent that Tom was dealing with some significant self-esteem issues. Specifically, he felt that he deserved to be playing much more than he currently was and that, since he was not, he must be a "loser." Because he was convinced he was a "loser," he didn't want to be seen in public, which translated into missing classes and isolating himself in his room before and after practice.

Tom had never before experienced not being an integral part of any team to which he belonged. We discussed the entitlement issue of "deserving" to play and how this belief can be dysfunctional if one considers not playing to be a personal insult. We also discussed the issue of conditional acceptance and the dysfunctional aspects of the "I'm only a good person if I play often and well" attitude. We explored possible antecedents to both the entitlement issue and the conditional acceptance issue and discovered that those beliefs were ingrained in him early in life by a father who would refuse to speak to him if he did not play well and also by a number of coaches who had treated him in a similar fashion. Tom discovered that he always measured himself in terms of what he had done athletically rather than in terms of who he was as a total human being. Finally, we discussed the reality that much of a college athlete's experience is out of his or her hands. Tom had very little control over a coach's decision to play him and no control at all over being injured. What he could control was the amount of effort that he chose to apply toward accomplishing his personal, athletic, and academic goals.

Tom came to realize that he was more than just a football player and that he did have control over many important areas of his life. He felt that there were some important issues that he needed to deal with pertaining to his relationship with his father, but decided to pursue them at a later date.

Tom still has not played much, but he continues to do well academically and seems to be working well within the student athlete system. He no longer considers himself a "loser" if he is not playing regularly, but he still competes vigorously for that opportunity.

Discussion Questions

1. Do you as a counselor or human service professional agree with the intervention strategies? If not, what would you have done differently?

2. Using Tom as an example, how can counselors become more successful in assisting the student athlete in assuming more responsibility for his or her own academic, athletic, social, and legal actions?

3. What images or stereotypes do you have regarding student athletes? How might these interfere with your ability to work with athletes?

CASE STUDY by Victoria D. Coleman and Shirl A. Barker

ATHLETICS AND CAREER DEVELOPMENT: A RESEARCH MODEL

Mike was a junior at a regional university in the midwest. His major was communications, and he was a linebacker on the football team. During the fall semester, he took an upper-level history course as an elective. While he received extensive tutoring, and stated that he spent several hours each week at the study table, he was unable to successfully complete the course. After discovering that he had failed the history class, he immediately barged into the professor's office exclaiming that his chance of a professional career with the NFL had been ruined because of the "F."

Mike was referred for individual personal and career counseling. It was apparent to the counselor that he perceived himself almost solely as a prospective professional football player and that he had devoted his entire life to this dream. The framework for intervention was the model of career development for student athletes described in chapter 9. After the counselor was able to calm Mike down, she proceeded to explain the type of assistance she could provide. Her focus was on the self-assessment component of the model of career development for student athletes, as she strongly believed that it was important initially to help Mike identify his values, interests, abilities, and personality traits. Mike had not previously received extensive personal and career counseling, and he was unable to identify anything besides football as being important in his life. The counselor assisted Mike in understanding that his interests and skills in football could be transferred to many career opportunities that he had not previously considered. After three individual sessions, Mike felt better about himself and was able to approach the spring semester with more confidence. He decided to continue the counseling, although his sessions were sporadic due to his academic and athletic commitments. At the end of his junior year, Mike was able to identify several alternatives that he would pursue if he were not drafted by the NFL or another football league.

Discussion Questions

1. How does Mike's overall attitude interfere with his performance toward achieving an education? What would be the counselor's role in such a situation?
2. What are some value differences between student athletes and nonstudent athletes? How might these affect the process and goals of counseling?
3. How might you modify your counseling style in working with student athletes?

CASE STUDY *by Mary Mitchell Harris*

DEVELOPMENTAL BENEFITS OF ATHLETICS

Power learning strategies were developed to assist a group of student athletes to achieve success on a precalculus test. The success visualization technique used required the students to set specific goals for the test scores they desired. They then described in detail how they expected to receive word of their success, amplifying the positive emotions that would be engaged and dramatizing the way they would celebrate. This sequence was written, told to a peer, and then visualized repetitively over a period of several minutes. The student athletes were told to practice the sequence before going to sleep at night and again on the morning of, or a few hours before, the test. The afternoon after the test, their facial expressions showed that the test had not gone well. (Indeed, the test was a disaster for the entire class.) However, part of the success visualization was to return to class the following day to receive their test paper. They all were present the following day, and to their surprise the professor gave everyone present a 50-point bonus for being there. As a result, each student athlete who participated in the exercise received a score higher than the goal he or she had set. They were encouraged to celebrate their successes and not question why or how. Power learning techniques sometimes yield curious and unexpected benefits.

Discussion Questions

1. What should counselors know about the Power Learning Techniques Model in order to utilize it to successfully assist students in balancing academics and athletics?
2. Do you as a counselor or human service professional believe that this model's characteristics are more beneficial than others in terms of developing the whole student academically and athletically?
3. In applying the generic characteristics of counseling to counseling student athletes, which ones seem to be potential barriers? Why?

CASE STUDY *by Wyatt D. Kirk and Sarah V. Kirk*

THE AFRICAN AMERICAN STUDENT ATHLETE

Tony is a 21-year-old African American man currently playing semiprofessional basketball. On the surface Tony's life appears to be satisfactory; he is, after all, employed in the sport he loves. But Tony's future may hold little promise, because he was allowed to "slip through the cracks" in high school and college.

Tony was born and raised in the inner city of a large midwestern city. He grew up living with his mother, his two younger sisters, and an older brother who dropped out of school at age 16 and is unemployed. Tony, however, not only grew up but also grew tall, and by the time he was 16 he was 6 feet tall. He took full advantage of this natural gift to excel in what he came to love most—basketball. He dreamed of "becoming pro" and being another Magic Johnson. He became his high school's star player, and when he was not on the court at school, he could be found at his neighborhood basketball court, always pursuing his dream. Tony was able to avoid the pitfalls inherent in the drug environment that surrounded him.

However, Tony exerted little effort when it came to schoolwork. He attended class regularly but did not contribute, except in a social manner. He turned in few if any assignments and never took exams. Yet, because Tony brought trophies and honors to the school, he somehow received passing grades and finally obtained a high school diploma. While in high school, he was observed and recruited by many college representatives.

After Tony enrolled in a large, predominantly White university, the dream was shattered. As a college player, Tony was no longer the only "6-footer." His teammates were as skilled as he, and he was not always the highest scorer. The setting was unfamiliar, and he missed his family and friends. But most important, once in college Tony was expected to be not only an athlete but also a student. And Tony could not read or write.

Depressed, unhappy, and probably too embarrassed to share his secret or his pain, he did not seek help. Tutoring, counseling, and the other support services for athletes were not made available to him. He suffered in silence and alone.

Tony went where he "felt at home," and while associating with his new friends he began dabbling in drugs. Soon he was arrested and charged with "possession." Although he was not convicted, he dropped out of college and returned home. Currently, he talks of learning to read and write to "protect" himself, but in the meantime he is still trying to find his place and pursue his dream.

This is not an unusual scenario since, as reported in several chapters in this book, only 26% of African American male student athletes graduate from college. Stories such as Tony's raise grave concerns about the educational system and about support services for student athletes, particularly for African American student athletes. If the administrators, counselors, and teachers at Tony's high school had demonstrated greater concern for Tony's future, he might have been better prepared for the challenges of being a college athlete. If Tony and his mother had been advised by someone (i.e., a coach or counselor) with knowledge of the recruiting process, Tony might have chosen a college at which he would not have felt so isolated. Once Tony was enrolled at the university, he did not receive the support from coaches, advisors, and counselors that he needed. Because Tony's academic, personal, and social concerns were not attended to, he will now have to struggle to create a successful and fulfilling future for himself. His case, then, is testimony for the need for improved services for, and increased attention to, African American student athletes.

Discussion Questions

1. Should counselors possess some knowledge of African American culture prior to intervening with student athletes such as a Tony?
2. What could the school counselor have done to assist Tony in achieving his original dream or guide him toward pursuing a more realistic one?
3. Given the low number of African American student athletes who graduate from college (26%), what specific support services can be implemented to increase the overall graduation rate of this group?

CASE STUDY *by Wilford S. Bailey*

THE ROLE OF THE NCAA

In 1988, following an extensive institutional investigation, a university admitted or accepted responsibility for nearly all of the more than 40 violations found by the NCAA infractions committee. These violations primarily involved former members of the university's assistant football-coaching staff, a former athletic department academic counselor, and at least 14 representatives of the institution's athletic interests, one of whom was a former member of the university's board of regents. Violations included: (a) promises of large sums of money (e.g., $5,000 cash payment if the prospect would sign a National Letter of Intent to attend the university, a Nissan 300ZX automobile upon enrollment, and a $200 monthly allowance during the young man's attendance); (b) the provision of $5,000 to another prospect, delivered to his home after the young man signed a National Letter of Intent earlier that day; (c) arrangement for a third student athlete to receive an automobile provided at no cost by representatives of the university's athletic interest; (d) a monthly cash allowance ranging from $50 to $200 for yet another student athlete, paid over a period of about 20 months and provided or arranged by a former assistant football coach and representative of the university's athletic interests; (e) certification of eligibility for a student athlete to compete in three football games in 1984 when there was no official transcript on file for a course allegedly taken under a coach at another NCAA member institution, with the intent to use the course to meet the NCAA satisfactory-progress requirements; (f) the encouragement to a prospect by former university assistant coaches to provide false information during interviews with an NCAA investigator; and (g) the involvement of a former assistant coach who secured the enrollment of a highly visible prospect and arranged for such benefits as $5,000 cash upon signing the National Letter of Intent, multiple cash gifts averaging $125 during the first year of enrollment and $200 during the second year, and an expensive sports car at no cost to the young man, with the title being placed in the name of the young man's brother and with all payments for the car and for insurance being made by three representatives of the university's athletic interests.

Discussion Questions

1. What measures should be implemented to curtail these illegal actions?
2. Should the penalties be more severe for those who knowingly violate the rules, including the coaches, assistant coaches, and the students themselves?
3. What should counselors know about athletic rules and regulations (such as the NCAA governing policies) that they could share with student athletes in order to prevent them from getting into situations like those illustrated in this case?

CASE STUDY *by Karl B. Fields and Martha J. Delaney*

CONTROVERSIES IN SPORTS MEDICINE

Barbara, a college student and distance runner, first saw me for an uncomplicated metatarsal stress fracture. After evaluation I felt she should be able to complete the state championships even with this injury. We discussed the risks, and she quickly decided to go ahead with her race. I was impressed with her determination, and she went ahead to place third in the state championships. On her initial evaluation I could detect no physical abnormalities, form problems, or training errors that had caused her injury.

Over the next 3 years, as Barbara matured into a highly competitive collegiate runner, I subsequently saw her for two additional stress fractures and numerous other injuries. Although 50% of collegiate distance runners experience injury yearly, the frequency of Barbara's problems seemed excessive. Multiple evaluations by myself and several consultations with other physicians provided no physical evidence to explain why Barbara had so many problems.

As I got to know Barbara better, my understanding of her increased. On Type A screening tests Barbara scored at the highest level. Psychological evaluation revealed an extreme level of hostility, a tendency to punish herself for less-than-perfect performances, and a pattern of externalizing blame for any injuries (coaches giving the wrong workouts, roommates keeping her awake, trainers taping her improperly, etc.). These psychological factors led to behaviors that increased her injury risks dramatically.

Two behaviors that necessitated immediate intervention related to eating and training. When she raced badly, she blamed her poor performance on a perceived weight problem. She then would go on a 700-calorie diet, which was less than needed to replace the calorie expenditure of training. Such an extreme reduction in caloric intake clearly would increase her risk of bone breakdown and probably helps explain the multiple stress fractures.

The self-destructive training behavior tied directly into her competitiveness. When Barbara failed to meet the time expectations for a given workout, or when a runner she considered inferior finished ahead of her in training, she would punish herself with additional hard workouts. This type of extra stress caused her fatigue and pushed her to an overtrained state. Most years she ran well through the early races but experienced injuries before the important season-ending championship competitions.

The approach to dealing with Barbara's injuries that ultimately proved successful was counseling and careful monitoring of her training. She needed the help of a sports psychologist to deal with abnormal eating behavior and with the tendency toward self-punishment. The coaching staff cooperated with the sports psychologist by agreeing to give Barbara noncompetitive workouts on an every-other-day basis, which kept her from overtraining.

These strategies helped Barbara finish her senior year without injury and place in the South Eastern Conference championships. While sports medicine treatment helped her overcome individual injuries, prevention was impossible until the psychological factors in the etiology of her injuries were discovered. Counseling did not change Barbara's personality, but it did give her a program that allowed her to compete without adopting behaviors that clearly were harmful.

Discussion Questions

1. What should counselors know and understand about athletic competition and the intense pressure athletes place on themselves?
2. Since counseling did not change Barbara's personality, is ongoing counseling indicated to assist her in maintaining and controlling her destructive behaviors?
3. Are student athletes such as Barbara more susceptible to eating disorders and addiction than nonstudent athletes? How can counselors prevent this?

CASE STUDY *by George W. Schubert and Arline F. Schubert*

LAW AND SPORTS

J.R. was aggressively recruited from a small high school in the midwest where he was an outstanding student athlete who excelled in football. On the first day of the football signing period, J.R. signed a National Letter of Intent (NLI) with a Division I eastern institution.

After a short period at the eastern institution, where J.R. participated in football practice, J.R. realized he could not adjust to the cultural change and withdrew from the university. J.R. then enrolled immediately at a second Division I institution closer to his home. He requested permission from the eastern institution to contact the football coach at the midwestern institution.

Under the NLI agreement three actions could occur: First, the eastern institution could refuse to release J.R. from the NLI; J.R. would lose 2 years of eligibility and would be required to sit out for 2 years. Second, the eastern institution could release J.R. from the NLI, in which case J.R. would lose 1 year of eligibility and be required to sit out 1 year from football. Third, J.R. could request a waiver from the NLI Steering Committee, seeking elimination of any penalty. If the waiver were approved, J.R. would be subject only to conference and NCAA transfer rules.

When a student athlete signs an NLI and transfers to another institution during the first year's residency, precautions must be taken by those advising the student athlete to ensure that all alternatives and consequences are clear. In J.R.'s case, the third option was sought, the waiver was granted, and no further action was taken.

However, if an institution and/or the NLI Steering Committee refuses to release a student athlete, the only alternative may be to bring the matter before a court of law. A student athlete may contend that a former institution and the NLI unjustly impede his or her athletic experiences and progress. In a court of law a student athlete might file a complaint against the NLI Steering Committee and the signing institution arguing that the regulations promulgated and enforced by the NLI Steering Committee are excessive.

If it appears that the action of the NLI Steering Committee and the signing institution will cause future harm to the student athlete, then the student athlete may file for an injunction. An injunction is an extreme remedy and will be granted only if it appears that unless the Steering Committee is restrained from enforcing its decision irreparable injury will result. If the injunction is sought, the student athlete must be prepared to prove that the loss of eligibility is an unjust and excessive regulation and serves only to impede the progress of the student athlete in his athletic advancement.

Discussion Questions

1. What are some of the ramifications if a student athlete wants to break the agreement of the letter of intent? How can a counselor guide or advise the athlete in deciding what to do?
2. Ethically, what does the letter of intent mean in terms of the student athlete's responsibility in honoring it?
3. Ethically and legally, what does the letter of intent mean with respect to the institution's obligation to the student athlete?

CONCLUSION

Athletic and Academic Preparation for the Future

WYATT D. KIRK AND SARAH V. KIRK

The thrust of this book is twofold: presenting the proliferation of information (myths and realities) concerning selected issues that have an impact on academics and athletics, and providing information on, and discussions of, suggested models and strategies.

It is a hope that the human service professionals, coaches, professionals in sports medicine, and others who use this book will: (a) have a better understanding of the problems athletes face and (b) incorporate some of the listed skills and techniques into their own existing repertoire.

This treatise has explored three areas that can have a negative impact on all student athletes: athletic environment, issues that are special and unique to them, and the external forces that constantly touch their lives. The question now is, "Where do we go from here?" Are the problems facing our student athletes so devastating that there is no hope? Absolutely not! They myths have been shattered and the realities shared.

The next phase requires counselors and human service professionals to serve not only as practitioners but also as consultants in the athletic environment to ensure a more comprehensive and holistic approach to re-solving many of the problems facing these young people.

Academic and personal development of student athletes at the high school and especially at the college level is a growing concern among ad-ministrators, advisors, counselors, and student affairs personnel. Many of the problems involve academic, personal, and social dimensions and include a lack of individual self-identity and self-confidence outside athletics, un-realistic goals, deficiency of career plans, social isolation, alcohol and drug abuse, stress, and burnout. Effective models and strategies for sports counseling do exist and need to be used. These include career life planning and adapting frequently used counseling formats to sports counseling (Hinkle, 1989).

How well are student athletes prepared for the future when the idea of a professional sports career has been an indelible part of all past work, sweat, and dreams? The questions become (a) How well are athletes prepared for life? (b) How well are athletes prepared for another career? (c) What kinds of careers are they prepared for other than a career in professional sports? Frequently, we think of colleges and universities as places where students can and do accomplish certain developmental tasks and interact with peers in a learning environment. Jordan (1987) illustrated the student athlete's situation thus:

> However for the student athlete, he/she is put at a disadvantage in terms of development because of the training schedule, the practice schedule, and the actual game-playing schedule that most of them have to abide by in order to have playing time, in order to maintain their own ego (which has developed in the athlete, the student, and the person). (p. 2)

Student athletes are first and foremost individuals who are also involved in developmental growth, and academic and career program planning. The roles of student athletes have characteristically fallen into three areas: personal and social, academic, and athletic (Weston, 1984). They experience pressures that are different from those experienced by nonathletes and thus they have unique needs (Gordon, 1986; Schubert & Schubert, 1983).

The term *student athlete* is not inherently contradictory (Keihn, 1985). Unfortunately, however, there is a conflict that plays itself out when the athlete is unable to transcend role conflict or serve three masters (the academic role, the athlete role, and the personal and social role). Kirk (1991) conducted a survey exploring these three areas to ascertain the nature of programs in place (or plans) to assist athletes with career planning and, more important, personal and social adjustment.

THE NEED: ACADEMIC/ATHLETIC SURVEY

The main thrust of Kirk's (1991) survey was to establish whether institutions of higher education have a clear sense of obligation to the student athletes who are recruited. What are these obligations? Thomas and Ermler (1988) stated the following:

> Knowing that many athletes become absorbed in their cloistered athletic world at an early age and remain in it through the formative years when these life skills are developed in their peer group, one must look to the athletic establishment (including parents) to develop the skills that will permit a successful transition and retirement from sports. (p. 148)

Lee (1983) revealed that individual and group counseling need to begin prior to college enrollment. Schools that offer admission to a student athlete must provide the support needed to see the student through (Zahm, 1985; Zingg, 1982). Kirk's (1991) survey consisted of 80 questionnaires that were mailed to athletic directors at Division I colleges and universities. The survey dealt with revenue sports only, and included information regarding gender and race. A Holistic Model put forward by Lottes (1989) was the basis for the questionnaire, because Lottes had reported that no holistic support programs were available on university campuses. (Holistic was later referred to as "Whole-istic" [Lottes, 1991].)

Many of the respondents indicated that they did have programs that address academic, athletic, and personal and social areas, but not transition and retirement. There seems to be a number of advising and counseling programs in operation in colleges and universities, but there is no holistic support for student athletes. Most programs deal with one or two of the areas mentioned, using some of the following models that were mentioned in the survey (academic model, remedial model, developmental model, career model, injury model, drug model, counseling model, and a retirement model).

SURVEY OF CURRENT PROGRAMS

Academic Model

A total of 22% of Division I schools responding indicated that their school offers student athletes academic advising, academic monitoring, and academic assistance, primarily through the athletic department. Others use the career counseling programs that are available to all students. The remaining types of programs vary, including seminars, career development programs, and the athletic department's advising of athletes (Gurney, 1983). Athletic departments' advising of athletes has been criticized as impeding the athletes in attainment of their degrees. Wilkes, Davis, and Derer (1989) studied an athletes' educational planning program, and found that it initially focused on providing traditional study skills. After 2 years of operation, however, the researchers found that study skills programs were addressing only a portion of the athletes' academic needs. Programs targeted for student athletes that do not take into consideration the academic and athletic environment in which they exist are doomed to failure. Leach & Conners (1984) suggest that the adjustment of the student athlete may be attributed to academic support systems that stress intervention and sensitive advising. (This suggestion was supported by Jordan and Denson [1990], as well as Petitpas, Danish, McKelvam, and Murphy [1992].) One such program that proved effective is "Athletes and Academics" at Whitehaven High School in Memphis, Tennessee (see chapter 3).

Remedial Model

Less than 50% of the respondents indicated that there were remedial measures being used at their institution. A total of 35% do not use the remedial model, and others gave no response. Remedial programs, according to current literature, are used mainly with freshman student athletic programs. The remedial model identifies those student athletes who may be at risk or at high risk and who must compensate for deficiencies in order to increase their chances of completing their degrees. Petitpas and Champagne (1988) feel that all or most student athletes are at risk, especially freshmen. Students often enter college with a stereotypical worldview. Thus the goal for the freshman year is to involve athletes in a self-exploration experience so they may begin to move into more multidimensional thought. Although many of these programs may be for freshmen, this assistance may be needed beyond the freshman year. Caffey (1983) indicated that treatment beyond one semester was necessary to produce changes.

Developmental Model

No colleges or universities in Kirk's (1991) survey reported that they have developmental programs that deal with the unique psychosocial dynamics of student athletes. Review of the literature reveals that the developmental concept as a part of sports counseling is just coming into its own. Most counseling programs still center on academic needs or career development programs. Petitpas and Champagne (1988) have called for an increase in psychosocial programs, pointing out the unique needs of student athletes.

Career Model

According to responses to Kirk's (1991) survey, career development and planning programs are by far the most widespread. These programs deal with pre-career counseling and development rather than actual career opportunities after a professional sports career (Nelson, 1983). Intercollegiate athletes who have some unrealistic career goals and aspirations and lower levels of persistence to graduation, may derive many benefits from career counseling. Lee (1983) reported that 36% of the respondents in the subgroup of African American starters responded that they expected to become professional athletes, compared to 14% of the White starters, 11% of the African American nonstarters, and 8% of the White nonstarters. These data support current thinking regarding the unrealistic expectations that African American athletes have about future professional sports careers. Career programs at all levels might be of particular assistance to African American athletes, given their unrealistic expectations (see chapter 12).

Injury Model

Injuries represent a serious threat to an athlete's future. In Kirk's (1991) survey, none of the respondents indicated that their institutions had counseling programs to assist injured athletes, even though the athletes face injury regularly, perform in an environment that puts them at risk, and injuries could end a promising career. Little (1969) identified the "athletic neurotics" and cautioned that an individual's exclusive and excessive emotional dependence on any activity can place him or her in a highly vulnerable state and may lead to severe emotional consequences in the event or threat of unexpected termination. A model for athletic injury counseling should be given serious consideration.

Drug Model

None of the respondents indicated that there were any programs of drug counseling on their campuses for athletes. Some athletes use performance-enhancing drugs, such as anabolic steroids, as well as alcohol, and other drugs to combat problems like stress and burnout. Serious consideration should be given to assisting the athlete in understanding the role of drugs in athletics. One such program at Temple University, titled "Deter" (Farrell, 1987), has as its goal prevention of problems, as well as an ongoing educational component coupled with counseling sessions.

Counseling Model

Of the respondents 22% indicated that some type of counseling service was available to student athletes, primarily through campus agencies (in addition to the athletic department). Student athletes are referred for academic concerns, personal and social concerns, and career counseling. The remaining respondents gave no rationale for not having counseling available. The potential benefits of counseling for student athletes has been documented, and counseling should be a part of any holistic model of counseling for student athletes.

Retirement Model

None of the respondents indicated that their college or university had any type of counseling program that dealt with transition or retirement for student athletes. Given the importance of this issue (because the majority of student athletes do not go on to a professional athletic career) it would seem almost mandatory that a counseling program, or a life-after-athletics program, or another program dealing with career choice should be available and the student athletes should be encouraged to avail themselves of such a service. The athlete must focus on retirement when eligibility is exhausted, if he or she is injured, or if he or she fails academically. This type of sudden change has been linked to grieving. The experience and pain are often similar to the grief caused by the loss of a loved one. Thus anticipating retirement is an important part of counseling the student athlete (Rosenberg, 1984).

Advising and counseling programs in the colleges and universities primarily provide academic support to student athletes in the form of assistance with course selection, and tutoring and study tables. There is no "typical" model of advising and counseling student athletes on college campuses. We agree with Lottes (1989), who suggests that because there are so many interrelated issues involving the student athlete a holistic approach is needed to advising and counseling in all areas. There is a need to strengthen support services for student athletes and to consider the whole person. The holistic approach can help athletes in their sports participation specifically and help them make the transition once their professional sports career is behind them.

FUTURE IMPLICATIONS

Sports counseling realities call for professionals who can effectively address the needs of student athletes. Counseling student athletes is one of the most formidable challenges facing counselors and other professionals in human development. Meeting this challenge means counselors must be sensitive to the appropriate interventions for student athletes. New directions and practices are required, such as the holistic model discussed in this book, to better serve the student athlete as a whole person. "Why counselors?" some ask. Counselors have many skills that can be used effectively to address the needs of student athletes (career- and life-planning skills, communication-training skills, interpersonal relationship skills, assessment and appraisal skills, and stress-management skills). Moreover, as Remer, Tongate, and Watson (1978) stated in their discussion of the need for a counselor's involvement with athletes:

> The task is difficult. It is not impossible. It will take time and a great deal of patience. Counselors have been trained in values clarification and interpersonal dynamics, in recognizing and respecting alternate frames of reference, and in giving personal support. All these skills are necessary for entering the system, offering support, and handling defensive reactions. People with such skills are now being sought by those within the system. (p. 628)

More recently, the counseling concept has been put forward as indispensable at the high school level by Goldberg (1991) and at the intercollegiate level by Lanning (1982). Nevertheless, more training is still needed.

In the future, the challenge will be to add appropriate models and methods of education and treatment related to the practice of sport counseling. The holistic concept discussed in this book is just one example of what we can offer as professionals. In our experience as teachers, coaches, and advisors and counselors, we have come to see that a holistic approach is going to be of more use to athletes after athletics. In this way we all can assist the total person and enhance their sense of well-being.

Last, what is ahead as we look to the turn of the century and beyond? All of us in the human service area and sports community will need to assist our student athletes in keeping academics and athletics in perspective. We must help them understand the importance of keeping their identity and integrity while they negotiate the system and pursue a worthy career, be it in professional sports or—someday—in a career beyond the field of play.

References

Caffey, C. A. (1983). A study of the effects of group counseling on self-esteem, attitude and reading efficiency of athletes at the University of Mississippi. *Dissertation Abstracts International, 44,* 1728A.

Farrell, C. S. (1987). Temple's model drug education program includes tests but emphasizes counseling. *Chronicle of Higher Education, 33*(24), 35–36.

Goldberg, A. D. (1991). Counseling the high school student-athlete. *The School Counselor, 38,* 332–339.

Gordon, R. L. (1986). Issues in advising student-athletes. *NACADA Journal, 6,* 81–86.

Gurney, G. S. (1983). Athletic academic counseling within N.C.A.A. Division I institutions: A national profile of staffing, training and service. *Athletic Administration 17*(3), 9–13.

Hinkle, J. S. (1989, Fall). ACES sports counseling interest network formed. *ACES Spectrum, 50,* 8.

Jordan, J. (1987). *Academics, athletics and the student athlete.* Paper presented at the American Association for Counseling and Development Annual Convention, New Orleans.

Jordan, J. N., & Denson, E. L. (1990). Student services for athletes: A model for enhancing the student-athlete experience. *Journal of Counseling & Development, 69,* 95–97.

Keihn, D. J. (1985). Balancing academics and athletics: It's not an impossible task. *Chronicle of Higher Education, 30*(6), 88.

Kirk, W. D. (1991). *Academic/Athletic Survey.* Unpublished manuscript, North Carolina A&T State University, Greensboro, NC.

Lanning, W. (1982). The privileged few: Special counseling needs of athletes. *Journal of Sport Psychology, 4,* 19–23.

Leach, B., & Conners, B. (1984). Pygmalion on the gridiron: The Black student-athlete in a White university. In A. Shriberg & F. R. Brodzinski (Eds.), *Rethinking services for college athletes* (pp. 31–49). San Francisco: Jossey-Bass.

Lee, C. (1983). An investigation of the athletic career expectations of high school student athletes. *The Personnel and Guidance Journal, 61,* 544–547.

Little, J. C. (1969). The athletic neurosis: A deprivation crisis. *ACTA Psychiatric ACAND, 45,* 187–197.

Lottes, C. R. (1989). *A holistic model of counseling student-athletes on academic, athletic and personal issues.* Unpublished doctoral dissertation proposal, West Virginia University, Morganton, WV.

Lottes, C. R. (1991). "A whole-istic" model of counseling student-athletes on academic, athletic, and personal-social issues. *Counseling college student-athletes: Issues and interventions.* Morgantown, WV: Fitness Information Technology, Inc.

Nelson, E. S. (1983). How the myth of the dumb jock becomes fact: A development view for counselors. *Counseling and Values, 27,* 176–185.

Petitpas, A., Danish, S., McKelvam, R., & Murphy, S. (1992). A career assistance program for elite athletes. *Journal of Counseling & Development, 70,* 383–386.

Petitpas, A. J., & Champagne, D. E. (1988). Developmental programming for intercollegiate athletes. *Journal of College Student Development, 29*(5), 454–460.

Remer, R., Tongate, R. A., & Watson, J. (1978). Athletes: Counseling the overprivileged minority. *The Personnel and Guidance Journal, 56,* 616–629.

Rosenberg, E. (1984). Athletic retirement as social death: Concepts and perspectives. In M. Theberge & D. Donnelly (Eds.), *Sport and the sociological imagination: Referred proceedings of the 35th annual conference of the North American Society for the Sociology of Sport, Toronto, Canada* (pp. 245–258). Fort Worth, TX: Texas Christian University Press.

Schubert, G. W., & Schubert, A. F. (1983). A trilogy of academic concerns for the academic advisor of student athletes: General advising, litigation and NCAA proposal number 48. *NCDA Journal, 3,* 11–22.

Thomas, C. E., & Ermler, K. L. (1988). Institutional obligations in the athletic retirement process. *Quest, 40,* 137–150.

Weston, L. N. (1984). Identifying problems and accommodating needs of football student athletes at the University of Pittsburgh. *Dissertation Abstracts International, 45,* 1303A.

Wilkes, S., Davis, L., & Derer, L. (1989). Fostering career development in student athletes. *Journal of College Student Development, 30,* 567–568.

Zahm, D. (1985). The student-athlete: A tutor's perspective. *Athletic Journal, 66,* 48–49, 59.

Zingg, P. J. (1982). Advising the student athlete. *Educational Record, 63,* 16–19.

INDEX